THE

Perfect

BALANCE

THE

Perfect

BALANCE

HOW TO GET
AHEAD FINANCIALLY AND
STILL HAVE A LIFE

HANNAH McQUEEN

ALLEN&UNWIN
SYDNEY·MELBOURNE·AUCKLAND·LONDON

First published in 2012

Allen & Unwin
Sydney, Melbourne, Auckland, London

83 Alexander Street
Crows Nest NSW 2065
Australia
Phone: (61 2) 8425 0100
Fax: (61 2) 9906 2218
Email: info@allenandunwin.com
Web: www.allenandunwin.com

A catalogue record for this book is available
from the National Library of New Zealand

ISBN 978 1 877505 18 8

Internal design by Brittany Britten
Set in 11.5/16 pt Sabon by Post Pre-press Group, Australia
Printed and bound in Australia by Griffin Press

10 9 8 7 6 5 4 3 2 1

To my boys

Contents

Preface

ACHIEVING THE PERFECT BALANCE IS SIMPLE, IT'S JUST NOT EASY.

Myth: the more money you earn, the easier it is to get ahead.

There's an old saying, 'Money doesn't buy happiness'. No. But it certainly helps.

Money is supposed to help you live the life you want and allow you to reach your financial goals pre- and post-retirement. Yet this perfect point of balance eludes most people. Instead, many of us incorrectly assume that the two ideas are incompatible. We too easily accept that if we want to enjoy our lives, our financial goals won't be achieved, or if we commit to our financial success, we are not going to be able to do the things we love.

Many of us presume that the more money you earn, the easier it is to get ahead. However, those of us who enjoy higher incomes realise quickly that income levels and financial progress do not go hand in hand. Getting ahead has less to do with income and more to do with sustainability, the ability to keep going. To keep going you need to feel like you are living a life you enjoy, otherwise your momentum will wane fast. Finding the perfect balance is when you achieve that very precise point of having a life and getting ahead as fast as your circumstances allow.

MANAGING MONEY IS SIMPLE, IT IS JUST NOT EASY

Money is important in our lives, yet most of us gloss over it. Many books, when talking about wealth creation and getting ahead seem to brush lightly over our understanding of, and our ability to control, the basics of money. They presume we are already in control of our finances, or that we should be. For most people, this is not the case. Interestingly, if we could master the basics of money management then many wealth creation techniques would not be required.

It isn't that easy. Implying that we all should have our money sorted *and* that managing money is an easy thing to do is simply misleading. For many people, money is a complex subject. Often it is intrinsically linked to self-worth, and self-esteem. It plays a significant part in our lives and relationships, yet we never really discuss it openly with others, except to complain about increasing petrol prices or the price of milk. Sometimes in a crisis, we may discuss the state of our finances, but it is not a topic for everyday conversation.

Not discussing money and not talking about how much we earn is one of life's long-standing unwritten rules. Society once thought it vulgar to discuss the subject even though it is used to indicate how successful we are. In modern times, most of us continue to keep it private—it is personal, after all.

We don't want to introduce the money dynamic into relationships where it doesn't already exist. However, there is a risk that you may be in denial about how well you are doing financially or, if you are less confident with money, you may believe that money is bigger than you. Both these beliefs are dangerous.

People can feel frustrated and intimidated by money—it can even cause anxiety and stress. Many of my clients often complain that, despite earning more money than they have ever earned before, they do not have a sense of getting ahead any faster. The idea of finding the perfect balance between lifestyle and financial progress eludes them. They simply accept this as their current and future reality.

If left unchecked, holding onto misconceptions about money can become like a disease with an extensive reach. The stress of your relationship with money can affect your health and your other relationships, especially your intimate relationships. Whether you have a lot of money or not much, it's difficult to escape its reach.

Back in the day, marriage was a financial transaction. Today, marriage tends to be more about falling in love, finding a soulmate and spending more than you should on a wedding. I am all for finding your soulmate, but you need to think about what drives a long-term partnership. Although it can help to have similar money values, it is not critical. I have worked with people across the spectrum, from shopaholics to manic savers. I have worked with a married couple, one of whom was a prolific shopper and the other an assiduous saver, yet because they grew to accept their different money personalities, money wasn't an issue.

One of the partners suggested things worked nicely—one of them brought in the money, and the other spent it. It is not common, though, for such diverse money personalities to have so little conflict.

In the above situation, while the acceptance of each other's money personality was good for the relationship, little progress was being made towards the couple's financial capability. Equally, even clients more aligned in their money personalities can be unhappy with their financial position. The money comes in, and the money leaves almost as quickly. Unfortunately, elevating the role of money in a relationship isn't enough to create sustainable change (although it is a good first step). More often than not, confronting issues can either cause deep frictions in the relationship, or lead to heads being buried deeper in the financial quicksand.

Irrespective of your money values, you have to be able to work together to make sure you are getting what you need from your finances. You both need to be living a life you want and still be on track to achieve your financial goals. Shared financial goals are more important than shared money values.

Many of my clients surprise me, at least initially, with their ambivalence towards money. People tend to take a hands-off approach to managing their money. It is as if they think that somehow everything is going to be alright. As if someone, at some stage, is going to come and rescue them financially—cue 'Rich spouse with trust fund'. For most of us, this won't happen, yet we don't wake up and acknowledge this until retirement is a hair's breadth away. By then, it may be too late.

Being financially competent takes planning and planning takes time. To be successful, planning needs to be based on rational thought and decisions need to be made without emotion. Then you need to refine your plan to better reflect your situation. After that, you need to take more time, and you need to develop understanding coupled with accountability to get real results. If you are time-poor, you need to outsource your planning. Lack of time is an obstacle to getting ahead, but it is not an excuse for not making any progress.

Money issues are inescapable. Money changes things between people. Unaddressed money issues can cause stress and anxiety. Don't think that you are the only one having difficulty—many people are going backwards, they just don't realise it yet. On the other hand, well-considered and refined attitudes to money can create happiness and self-worth.

Today, overspending is of epidemic proportions, across society and generations. The overspending tends to be more 'about me' the younger the person is. As we get older and become parents and grandparents we still overspend, just less on ourselves and more on loved ones. A tendency to be generous with ourselves or others (that is, to be comfortable spending money on ourselves or others) is widely accepted, more so than ever before. I think that because we are all so time-poor, we look to 'make good' our relationships and our own wellbeing by spending money to buy convenience or to offset lack of time (to invest in relationships). Parents spend more money on their kids because it buys them a result. Individuals do it, businesses do it and governments do it. In New Zealand it is easy to overspend. On average, we spend all of what we earn. Prior to the global financial crisis (GFC), we were spending up to 10 per cent more than, we were earning. There are some valid reasons for this—some are within our control and some are outside our control. For example, high property prices compared to income levels are a factor outside our control. However, the ease with which we can overspend on frivolous items is a factor we can control. The idea of sticking to a budget is easy enough, so why are there so few people that can do it?

My team and I have worked with just over 2000 New Zealanders—young, old, self-employed and salaried—to help them find the perfect balance between a life well lived and maximum financial progress made. Some are in relationships, some are single. Some have children, some don't. Several are financially literate, a few aren't. Some are thinking about retirement, others are fresh out of school. They all want to get ahead faster and, irrespective of each person's position, three consistent themes have emerged:

- Number one—You are never doing as well as you think you are.

- Number two—It is never too late to change your financial landscape, but you have to start, and you need a watertight plan.

- Number three—Achieving the perfect balance is simple but not easy, and anything that suggests otherwise is a myth.

If this book achieves nothing else, it will give you

encouragement and permission to be honest about your finances and it will help you make the right start to get ahead faster.

MY BACKGROUND

I'm an accountant with a Masters degree in tax. Although my husband did not study money or business, he is Scottish (and therefore less inclined to spend money, just like the clichés suggest). When we graduated from university, we had a combined income of $32,000. We thought we were the richest people in the world. Fast forward eight years to us earning almost ten times that income, and we didn't feel better off. If anything, we felt we were on a treadmill that required us to keep earning more money just to maintain the status quo. This treadmill had us running faster and harder. We certainly weren't taking a stroll as I had always hoped.

To purchase our first home we needed a mortgage of $350 000. Until then, I never thought that money was a dynamic in our relationship—we always seemed to have enough and we never argued about it. With hindsight, I realise we had fostered a dynamic of indifference towards money. We were both relaxed about money—too relaxed. It came in and we presumed it would keep coming, but just as quickly as it came in, it left us.

To raise that mortgage I did what everyone does—I played the banks off against each other to try and get the best interest rate. I did get a good interest rate, but strangely, to me at least, the actual value of the savings was very little compared to the outgoings over the life of the mortgage. Sure it saved about $20 000 over the life of the mortgage and, of course, I would prefer that money in my pocket as opposed to the bank's. However, I was going to be paying back the $350 000 originally borrowed and a massive $490 000 in interest costs to the bank over the next 30 years!

I became fixated on understanding how to save more of the total interest cost. I kind of understood that compound interest was making the interest cost so high, but I didn't know how compound interest actually works, and I didn't understand how to circumvent it.

I understood that the longer I had my mortgage or owed money to the bank the more it was going to cost me. So, to save myself interest I needed to repay my mortgage faster. How could I do this without having my mortgage dictate my lifestyle?

After posing this question, I started to diddle with the calculus around how to structure my debt, based on my unique situation, in order to repay it faster. I only studied calculus until second year at uni so I didn't get very far. So, I decided to call my old university to see if someone could help me solve the problem.

I met with Dr Jamie Sneddon, a calculus tutor. I don't know what defines a genius, but I am sure he comes close. A few months and a fair few pages of calculus later, we had written a formula for structuring debt to repay it as fast as circumstances allow, while living the lifestyle you enjoy. The formula calculates the perfect balance every time.

However, it does make one key assumption—that you

will have money left over at the end of the week, month or year that can be used to repay your debt faster. It seems a reasonable assumption, but when I started thinking about my own situation I realised I was living from one payday to the next and I did not have much in the way of savings. There were times when I couldn't repay my credit card in full (usually after an overseas holiday). It was ironic that I had this incredible formula, but it was worthless until I could solve the first problem of where all the money was going. How could I find the money while continuing to live a lifestyle I enjoy? Could I get ahead faster without compromising that lifestyle? Could I find a perfect balance?

Chatting to my friends I discovered I was not the only one caught on this treadmill—most of my friends said they felt the same way. A lot of the people I spoke to were accountants, CEOs and the like—educated people who work with numbers and money on a day-to-day basis—yet they were not making much progress on a personal level.

I wanted to understand why and I wanted to apply my formula to the problem, so I started my company enableMe Ltd—financial personal trainers—to help solve this problem. Here, I reveal some of the secrets we have learned and mastered to help you find the perfect balance faster.

Introduction

Money is a funny thing. The mere word seems to intimidate people and many switch off or disengage when talk turns to finance. Understanding money is a much-needed life skill that you must master for your own benefit, for your children's benefit and for the benefit of your personal relationships.

To be money smart is to be socially responsible. Let's face it, most things, either directly or indirectly, are linked to money. To understand money properly, forget everything else you have been taught. Don't let yourself be intimidated by the numbers—the numbers are simple and the logic is simple. It's in the application, the actual doing, that most people come unstuck. Too many people make the mistake of thinking that because the principles are simple to understand, they will be easy to apply.

Media and even professionals often use flippant language to imply that getting ahead is easy. This makes people feel stupid for not mastering it, but getting ahead is not easy, otherwise we would all be doing it. We definitely wouldn't be in a recession.

The current recession has been brought about because we are all spending more than we earn, businesses are spending more than they earn and governments around the world are spending more than they earn. One of the cutest explanations a client gave to explain her financial situation was, 'I am Spain, and my husband is more France.'

So many of my clients, who would be described as smart Kiwis earning great money, describe themselves as 'floating', not 'flying'. And this is the crux of the problem.

You need to appreciate how you relate to money and the role money plays in your relationships. This book goes beyond strategies for solving immediate money problems and focuses on the mechanics of managing money (conscious finance) and your relationship with money (subconscious finance). If you can master both types of finance, money can start to play the right part in your life. It's a tool—one of the most valuable tools you can have.

As an adult, looking back on my childhood, I remember being taught to respect God, my elders and the sea. I don't recall ever being taught to respect money. Studying commerce and law, I was taught to revere certain laws, but never money. However, money does need to be respected as the means to help you build a lifestyle you enjoy, which will lead to building a satisfying and happy life.

Have you ever had any of the following thoughts?

- If I want to make progress, I will have to give up my lifestyle.

- I earn good money, but don't feel like I am getting ahead as fast as I should.

- I do not believe I should have to give up my lifestyle to get ahead.

- I feel like I am on a treadmill with my finances—the

money I have earned just seems to have created a bigger wheel which I need to keep turning.

- I am the breadwinner—the buck stops with me, but I am not sure if I can be doing it smarter.

- I competently work with money as my job, but still struggle to get ahead personally.

- I know I need to think about retirement, but I am not sure where to start or whether I have left it too late.

- I am self-employed, earning good money and I can put a lot of my personal costs through my business, yet my finances are still a mess, and I feel that everything has just morphed into one, and I am still not getting ahead any faster.

- I am nervous for my children—have I taught them enough about money?

- My partner and I do not always agree about money.

- How am I supposed to pay for my retirement?

The best investment you can ever make is in yourself. Please, take some time and let me teach you about money.

Chapter 1

Let's get started

There are four things you need to understand if you are going to achieve financial success. They are:

- Subconscious finance—the psychology of your spending habits

- Conscious finance—your financial smarts

- Your capability to optimise the decisions you make about money

- How to build momentum and get the results you want.

It is not easy to get ahead and it is even harder to get ahead as fast as you possibly can. However, before we can change your financial future we need to understand where you are now and why you are there. Always remember, the only person that will truly ever care about your money is you. Burying your head in the sand is no longer an option.

Forget about maths, interest rates and the recession. Forget about your bills, your mortgage, how old you are and how many years until retirement. Think about the following:

- Where do you want to be, financially?

- Where are you now, financially?
- What are the obstacles preventing you getting there?

WHERE DO YOU WANT TO BE?

If you do not know where you are going, you will end up some place else. — Yogi Berra

Individual goals vary from person to person, but we all need to aspire to being financially successful. Not rich—that is optional—but successful. I define financial success as being able to live a lifestyle you enjoy, free of anxiety and stress around money. For me, it means that you are mortgage-free, or well on the way to being mortgage-free, and you have your retirement sorted. Incorporated into 'living a lifestyle you want' are the micro goals of being in control of your money, not having to earn more money to get ahead, having a rainy-day fund, being able to replace your car when you want to, taking holidays when you want to and buying property when you want to.

To be financially successful is to be 'flying' financially. The reality for many people is they don't even feel like they are getting ahead on a day-to-day basis. The thought of being successful is not even on their radar. With this book, I hope that will change.

> **Financial success is not linked to earnings. It is linked to progress.**

The end point is the same for everyone—to 'fly' financially. But before we can work out how to get you to this point, we need to establish where you are now. Are you sinking, floating, or flying?

WHERE ARE YOU NOW?

There is nothing noble about being superior to some other man. The true nobility is in being superior to your previous self. — Hindu proverb

Finding the balance financially has less to do with understanding maths and commerce, and more to do with understanding your natural tendencies and how your spending psychology works. You need to appreciate how you relate to money and the role money plays in your relationships on a conscious and subconscious level. If you can master this, money can start to play the right part in your life. Money is a tool. It's one of the most valuable tools you can have.

Have you ever had to hop on scales in front of someone? Have you noticed you tend to weigh more than you think? Just as we tend to weigh more than we think, we are usually not doing as well as we think financially. We are disconnected from the reality of our financial position, and we are often disconnected from the impact of our own financial behaviour.

ARE YOU FLYING, SINKING OR FLOATING?

Flying means different things to different people. Let's assume at the very minimum it encompasses you being able to live a lifestyle you enjoy, you being well on the way to repaying your mortgage, if you have one, your retirement being sorted and you having no stresses around money.

Some people fly higher than others, but how high you fly also relates to your stomach for risk, which we will discuss later.

> If you are not flying, then you are either sinking or floating.

Sinking means you are going backwards, or you are always on the back foot. Your back is up against a wall and no matter how you try it always feels tight. You tend to use debt, or credit cards, when life throws you a curve ball. You do this because you do not have a rainy-day fund. You do not always clear your credit cards each month. If you were to complete a true budget of how much money is coming in each month versus what you are spending, you would probably find that you are spending more than you earn. Another sign this may be the case is if you get a payrise but it doesn't make a difference because it gets used for your day-to-day living costs.

It is common in a relationship where one partner manages the money for the party managing the finances to feel as if they are sinking, whereas the person removed from the money feels as if they are floating. People on commissioned or irregular income may feel that they are sinking at various points of the year.

When you are sinking you tend to put purchases you cannot afford on credit. The purchase may feel good initially; for example, booking a holiday you can't afford, but this feeling rapidly wears off. Your overspending will catch up with you. Even if you can keep your creditors—the people you owe money to—at bay, it will eventually take its toll on your health and relationships. This is not the way to live.

Not surprisingly, people who are sinking do not set out to be in this situation. It usually starts slowly with being on the back foot. A curve ball throws you backwards again, and before you know it, you are picking up momentum in the wrong direction, again. Many self-employed people or people with commissioned income sit on the cusp of sinking as their irregular income can cause havoc with their finances. This is not the way to live and I would encourage them to develop a plan to help smooth out the ebb and flow of their income. I do not believe that past results indicate your future capability.

If you are the money-managing partner in a relationship and have a feeling that you are sinking, your partner needs to be made aware of and agree with, or at the very least acknowledge, your diagnosis. You need to share a strong desire to fix the situation otherwise there is no point in trying.

Where your personalities are such that one is more 'entrepreneurial, big-picture, broad-brush, it's going to be okay in the end', and the other prefers to deal with the 'right here and now, nuts and bolts' of managing money, you may never agree on your financial position because in accepting the diagnosis the entrepreneur can feel that you are not believing in them.

I do not bother seeing a new client if relationship finances are a problem unless both partners attend. It is never one person who is responsible for the problem and it will never be one person in a relationship who can fix it. When I set about fixing this sort of situation I often have to take a drastic, slash-and-burn approach. Clear the decks, suck it up, sell assets, stop spending and let's turn this situation around.

Working to a tight plan, you have about six months to turn a situation around. After that, people lose momentum and start to slide backwards again. So, the first plan has to work and get immediate results, otherwise you might as well hang up the gloves before you even start. In that six-month period, the sole objective is to get to a floating position. Then, as soon as people are floating the goal posts need to change.

> **Tip: Not sinking as fast as you were does not mean that you are floating.**

Floating is when you are not going backwards, but you are not getting ahead particularly fast. You may be earning the most money you have ever earned, but you don't feel better off.

Most of my clients initially sit in this category. They are living a comfortable lifestyle, but are living from payday to payday. If they were to lose their job tomorrow, they could probably survive a few weeks with available cash, and then use credit or access the equity in their property to get by. When they come to me they are not necessarily stressed about money but disillusioned that they are not making the progress they expected.

If you are in this situation you need to understand where the money is going. Knowing your actual spending patterns can help you identify the money that is being 'frittered', or lost. You need to maximise tax efficiencies and start structuring your debt—usually a mortgage—to repay it faster. You need to enjoy your lifestyle, accepting that you do not have to spend every dollar you earn to do so.

Having established a plan with my clients to get them ahead, we test it, refine it, track their progress, and as they stick to the plan consistently, they start to pick up momentum. Usually after twelve months, they get some wind beneath their wings and start to fly, maybe slowly to begin with, but with each month will start flying higher and towards their destination faster.

Flying means more than having no money worries. It means being on track to achieve your financial goals that, at the very least, incorporate being able to live a lifestyle you enjoy and fund your retirement. Flying is living in perfect balance.

If you are reading this book, I assume you are sinking or floating or, at the very least, not flying as high as you might like or in the direction you want to go. Many clients say they don't feel as if they are going backwards, but there is no real sense of getting ahead. This creates a stress or frustration of sorts. Add this money dynamic to your personal relationships and you are in for a rocky ride, unless you and your spouse develop some money skills fast.

If you can diagnose your current situation, and you know the destination, you are almost there. Next you need to identify and understand your current obstacles to tailor a plan to overcome them in order to achieve your goals faster.

> **Tip: Money is a tool to get what you want—it's not the end goal.**

WHAT IS STANDING IN YOUR WAY?

If you can find a path with no obstacles, it probably doesn't lead anywhere. — Frank A. Clark

People seldom improve when they have no other model but themselves to copy. — Oliver Goldsmith

So if you know where you are at, and where you want to go, what is holding you back? Is it you? Is it your situation? Do you lack understanding or motivation? Is it a combination of these? Obstacles come in many different forms—from biology, psychology, relationships, and self-created walls.

Until you set about identifying why you are where you are, there is a higher chance you will repeat the same mistakes that led you to your current position.

COMMON OBSTACLES

I divide obstacles that might be standing in your way into three categories:

- Psychological obstacles

- Current situation

- Money traps.

As a combination, or in isolation, any of these obstacles can prevent you getting ahead as fast as you might. Each roadblock needs to be identified, so that it can be turned into a building block.

To identify psychological obstacles you need to look inward. They include your money personality, or your natural tendencies around money. Don't think that because you are rational in normal life you are rational around money, or that because you manage money as part of your job that you will be able to manage it well in your private life. I have found little connection between the two; for example, I know many accountants who are shopaholics.

YOUR MONEY PERSONALITY

There are essentially three money personalities:

- Shopper

- Saver

- Plodder—neither a shopper or a saver.

Some people fit the textbook description of one key personality, yet still have tendencies from other personalities. Others have been known to take these definitions to an extreme. Many people have never considered their relationship with money.

To help you identify your money personality ask yourself the following questions:

- Do I find it easier to spend money, or save money?

- Do I enjoy spending money?

- Am I rational with my money?

If you are in a relationship ask yourself the following questions:

- Does my partner agree with me about money matters?

- Are we financially compatible? (For more on this subject see Chapter 2 on money and relationships.)

Shoppers

Shoppers derive emotional satisfaction from spending money—they like to shop. Some shop to feel good, some shop to celebrate feeling good. Some shop for no reason at all. The instant satisfaction of buying something motivates them. I am probably a shopper. One of my favourite pastimes is spending money. My best weekends have involved illicit trips to Sydney or Melbourne for a 'quick fix'. The more money I earned, the easier I found it to rationalise my spending. The more I earned, the more generous I became, with myself and with others. A shopper doesn't always have to spend large amounts of money. Some feel it is their entitlement to spend money, so they do. It is common for this type of personality to work in high-stress jobs where a quick-fix purchase can buy instant reward or help them to keep working hard. Shoppers are often time-poor and will happily pay for convenience.

'Controlled shoppers', or 'bargain shoppers', disguise their tendency from themselves, as they spend very little on a day-to-day basis, but when it comes to one-off purchases— often around technology or toys—they hold nothing back.

Someone who can be fairly tight on a day-to-day basis— like my Scottish husband—will buy the best of a big-ticket item once they decide they want to buy something. This can be quite common in a male who is not as engaged in the running of a household. Generally, he may not spend much on himself, but when he decides he wants to buy a 'toy', he will happily go ahead and spend a large amount without any qualms. Some people spend on their children, or their house, and don't attach the same responsibility or guilt they might have if they spent the same amount of money on something for themselves. If you cannot afford to spend money, even if it is for a righteous endeavour, you cannot afford to spend it.

Not everyone is a shopper all of the time, yet overall shoppers find it easier to spend money than save it. Subcategories of the shopper include the comfort shopper and the binger.

Bingers

'Bingers' are created by natural tendency or by circum-stance. People who are self-employed or have an irregular income are more used to a feast-or-famine lifestyle. When there is no money they stop spending, but when the money is coming in thick and fast, usually from a big lump-sum payment, they spend as if there is no tomorrow.

The natural tendency of a binger is to be able to success-fully save for something. But in the absence of a clear goal, they are more inclined to spend their money on 'stuff'. Or they save, and then they splurge, sometimes spending more than what they have saved.

Comfort shoppers

A comfort shopper is just that. Some people eat food to derive comfort; some people shop. If you derive emotional satisfaction from the goods you buy or the process of pur-chasing them, then you might be a comfort shopper. You do not have to enjoy buying *all* things to be guilty of this pleasure, either—just some is enough to be classified a com-fort shopper.

> **Money spent is money spent.**

Savers

Savers derive more satisfaction from saving than spend-ing—generally they take little joy from spending money. They are quite happy to go without, and have a natural consciousness about money. A saver does not need to be industrious, just tight. Some cultures tend to be predisposed towards savings; for example, the Scottish and the Dutch. A Jewish client of mine said that he derives satisfaction from seeing his bank account grow—it gives him a small thrill. It is not enough for him to not spend—he wants to see his wealth grow. On the other hand, his European wife seems to get a similar thrill when she grooms her very expensive animals. Interestingly enough, in this relationship there were no arguments around money, but a general acceptance that things could be done better. They just needed to find out what to do so that they both got what they needed and could reach the perfect balance faster.

A lot of people incorrectly diagnose themselves as savers, when it is more appropriate to say that they are tight on a day-to-day basis. When it comes to buying something they like, or spending money on their hobbies, however, they happily make large lump-sum payments. Often, those big lump-sum payments equal, and at times outweigh, the small but frequent amounts their partner may have spent, even though they consider themselves more of a saver than their partner.

A lot of people have saved historically, or have saved for an event; for example, a wedding, and may therefore consider themselves savers. Using the analogy of fitness, being fit at some stage in your life doesn't mean that you can run a marathon right now.

> To be called a saver—or non-spender—
> saving must be a natural tendency and not
> take conscious effort.

Plodders

Plodders are ambivalent about spending and saving. They take things as they come and have an expectation that if they keep doing what they are currently doing, they should be okay. Typically, they will be okay while they are working, but plodders and an enjoyable retirement do not often go together. If you do not identify with the traits of the other personalities, it is likely you are a plodder.

PERSONALITY COMBINATIONS

Money is a powerful force in intimate relationships, because whether you have a lot of money or a little money, you never escape its reach. Although it can help to have similar money personalities, this is seldom the case, or a guarantee to success. Just as we have our quirks around money, so does our partner. With these differences, niggles tend to appear.

I am not sure if Freud had an opinion on this, but I have found that opposites seem to attract when it comes to money personalities. Or perhaps it is more correct to say that a couple could be aligned in their ambitions, world view, religion and basic life philosophy, yet might not consider the alignment of their money attitudes. Being unified on many core beliefs has no direct bearing on aligning your money matters. Ironically, money is seldom discussed during the 'getting to know you' stage of a relationship, yet it is one of the most common reasons why relationships end. More often than not, the shopper almost inherently falls for the saver (neither probably aware of the other's money tendencies at the time of falling in love). This creates a dynamic all in itself. A shopper married to a shopper—well, that can be a recipe for disaster. Or you may share my own relationship diagnosis, where you are both hands-off about money.

Whatever form your relationship's money dynamic takes, I have found that the money dynamic in a relationship almost inherently leads to elevated emotion. If left untreated, it will, inevitably, become the elephant in the room. When it is not talked about that elephant will affect your financial success and, probably, your relationship.

The shopper/shopper combination is always fun. They are having a good time, but not going far financially. It can be a dangerous combination as both tend to be in denial about their individual and combined levels of spending. They happily justify their own, and each other's, spending. They do not say no. There may be an underlying awareness that financial progress is not being made, but it is not of interest to either party to raise this issue. It is not uncommon for a shopper to be earning good money but spending it all, and more.

The saver/saver combination is rare. However, much like the shopper/shopper combo, it makes for comfort and compatibility. You might be getting ahead, but are you getting ahead fast enough, or could you do it better?

The shopper/saver combination, though common, can be also frustrating. One partner is trying to get ahead and the other is spending. Generally, the good—savings—of one is cancelled out by the bad—spending—of the other and overall they are making little to no progress. A niggle around finances, if not addressed, can become a bigger problem than it should be.

In many relationships, the saver does not manage the day-to-day spending, yet they have an opinion on how much should be spent and what it is spent on. Often, they are quick to point out when they think that too much has been spent. If you are a saver—a more conscious spender—be aware that highlighting genuine overspends to your partner does not always go down a treat, even if what you are saying is technically correct. The saver's opinion, even when it is valid, can be interpreted as judgemental and irrelevant.

Let's face it, who wants to be accountable to their spouse for finances? Like many things in a relationship, just because something is rational it doesn't mean that your partner wants to hear it from you.

Looking at weight loss, if I was to go on a diet and ask my husband to tell me if he thinks I could do things better, I know I would be offended if he told me I could do some component of the diet better, even if I had asked him to be honest with me. But if my personal trainer said the exact same thing to me, I would take it on board, listen and change my behaviour to reflect the advice. It is not because I disagree with my husband—it is because I don't want to be accountable to him. This attitude can be carried over to finances as well.

Most people do not want to be accountable to their spouses around money. Those days are long gone and most couples in the Western world don't want judgements being an undercurrent of their financial relationship. Savers will almost inherently suggest spending less on a particular item or service, but the shopper will not heed the advice. In some cases, the advice to cut costs might not be good advice for the item being purchased, although the basic idea was sound.

I am not siding with the saver—as a mother running a household, nothing frustrates me more than someone suggesting I should spend less on a particular item when they have no idea of the actual costs associated with the purchase in question.

A common example of this problem from my clients occurs around Christmas and birthday presents. Males in general have little idea about this area. It is not to say they don't have good ideas about how to keep costs down, but why would you listen to someone who is disconnected from the real costs of day-to-day living? Why should you spend less on something when you know that it will bring you happiness? (For more on this subject see the section on happiness in Chapter 2.) Putting money personalities to one side, most of us are not as rational and logical as we think.

Different money personalities in a relationship are common, although it doesn't mean that you can't have the same financial goals. Unlike differing personalities, different goals will be detrimental to financial success and will almost always obstruct your combined progress. If you are in a relationship where you both have differing financial habits or personalities, it is more common for the spouse with the poor habits to sabotage financial progress than for the more disciplined spouse to lift your results. However, irrespective of differing tendencies, you have to be able to work together to get what you both need from your finances. One spouse may need to feel that on a day-to-day basis they are making inroads on their finances and are on track to pay their mortgage off faster. The other spouse may care less about the mortgage and be more motivated about creating tax savings, or being able to replace their car sooner. Although your goals may vary, they should never clash or be mutually exclusive; otherwise you are going to run into trouble at some stage.

MONEY TRAPS

Whether it is our individual psychology, our relationships or sheer ignorance, more and more of us are falling prey to some pretty dumb traps to do with money. There are things happening in our subconscious that can upset even the most determined of us. As it turns out, our brains perform a number on us more than we realise. Researchers in the fields of neuroeconomics and behaviour economics dedicate their studies to the reasons how and why we behave certain ways with money. While I don't want to diminish their findings, you don't have to be a professor of neuroeconomics to understand and overcome certain money traps. However, before you can learn to sidestep a trap, you need to be able to see the trap for what it is. Whether or not you are personally susceptible to a money trap can be immaterial if your partner is ensnared by one. Increase your odds of success by avoiding these common dangers.

A money trap is not just making a decision you regret later. It is the trigger to the decision that you might later regret—or worse, repeat—because you are yet to latch on to the real outcome. A money trap is not buying a leaky building, or putting your money into a collapsed finance company, or some Ponzi scheme. Yes these are mistakes, but they are not the trap. A trap is more an obstinate belief you hold onto, or a financial law that you ignore. Financial beliefs are not designed to improve your moral compass, but they do have a huge sway on where you end up in life. If you feel you are making little progress financially, then it may be that you keep falling into money traps.

Ostrich effect

Burying one's head in the sand is one of the biggest threats to relationships and financial progress. Symptoms of this effect include procrastinating about taking financial action, and having a wad of unopened bills. It is common to suffer anxiety and helplessness around money. You feel getting ahead is beyond your control, so you ignore it completely and feign indifference. This indifference is usually masking a sense of inadequacy, failure and hopelessness, and this hopelessness often leads to denial and financial paralysis.

A lot of people believe that they lack a special talent when it comes to money. But while achieving the perfect balance is a skill that doesn't come naturally to most, it is a skill that can be learned, developed and honed.

Your financial situation impacts you whether you want to be aware of it or not. It is always better to know, in detail, what you are up against, so you can plan accordingly. It is time to get out of the sandpit, open the envelopes full of bills, find out what you owe and to whom, take responsibility and start moving forward.

Inertia—immobility

Just as you can teach your kids that someone else will always bail them out if things get too hard, some people accept their money problems as being bigger than them and think that, save their parents coming to their rescue, nothing can be done.

There is no financial problem so big that you have to relinquish control. Even bankruptcy, for all its hype, can in fact be an opportunity to clear the decks, take a breath and move forward faster. You might not know how to overcome your problem, but that in itself does not mean it cannot be overcome. As they say, if you chose to stick your head in the sand, watch out for the incoming tide.

I had a client who illustrated this perfectly. He worked in finance. In his personal life he kept trying to fix many financial failures—chronic debt, no savings, scant retirement funds, marriage breakdown—but he kept stumbling. He would make some inroads then take a step backwards just as quickly as he had moved forwards. Some of the stumbling was self-imposed; some of it came from being so far on the back foot that he was never able to right himself. No matter what good happened, it was absorbed by his day-to-day living, and each curve ball seemed to knock him back further. He needed to do two things simultaneously: he needed to stop spending and he needed to downgrade his house to reduce the mortgage payments that he had taken over when he separated from his wife. He should have sold the house and split the proceeds, and moved on, but he was not prepared to do this. Instead, he chose to demonstrate a self-imposed ignorance about all things financial. In the end he was the poster kid for 'someone else will save me'—the belief that you'll be rescued by someone or something, that if you just keep going somehow it will be okay. But this mindset stopped him doing what was necessary to fix the situation.

Without even realising it, people do things that jeopardise their financial success. All too often the shock of drastic change—whether it is a job loss, a relationship breakup, or a failed business—can paralyse you financially or trigger knee-jerk reactions. Remember, though, that these events do not determine your financial capability—it is your reaction to them that will.

> Nothing splendid will ever be achieved, unless you consider yourself superior to circumstance. [Bruce Barton]

Entitlement syndrome

So often, those who earn good money spend good money. They spend it because a part of them believes they can—because they believe that their income will continue indefinitely, or because of a belief that they work hard so they deserve to spend what they want when they want. They usually have enough money to cover their bills, so they are not confronted with slipping backwards or ever-increasing credit card balances. In fact, they may feel that they are responsible with money because of the lack of back-sliding. This belief could be reaffirmed if those around you are doing averagely. This complacency allows slippage and does not capitalise on or exploit the opportunity you have to get ahead faster. I speak from personal experience. As I moved up in the corporate world, earning more money seemed to give me permission not to worry about my money, instead of doing the smartest things with it.

The majority of the clients I work with, in fact, suffer from this syndrome to some extent. Very few of them are going backwards; instead, many are simply standing still, or not getting ahead as quickly as they could. A common illustration of this syndrome is when you comfortably, or automatically, pay your credit card in full each month, therefore incurring no interest on the purchases made. The ability to repay your credit card as it falls due reinforces your belief that you are doing well financially. Let's say you have around $3000 owing at the end of one month. You pay this in full before the due date, comfortably. However, the real question that is seldom asked is did you need to spend $3000; could you have spent, say, $2500, with the difference being 'slippage' because you are acting under a cloud of entitlement?

We have found those who work hard and earn good money not only rely on this to keep them from financial difficulty, but interpret this as financial success. Unfortunately you cannot use income as the sole measure of success, as this only considers one side of the equation. If you spend what you earn, you may look good, but you will still in fact be going nowhere. More often than not you will measure your success against your peers, who are likely to be living under the same illusion you are. A sense of entitlement usually leads to underperformance.

Anchoring

Anchoring is when you use the wrong reference point to guide your decision-making. For some, anchoring is a skill, and it is a known sales technique. For those making investment decisions, however, it can be a sign of stubbornness and could end up detrimental to your overall financial progress.

A clever salesperson will use anchoring to illustrate what a good deal you are getting. They will show you an item that costs more, and is perhaps not quite what you want, first. This creates a reference point, so that when you are shown the item you do want, you subconsciously compare it to the first item, feeling that you have snatched a bargain. Real estate agents play this tune time and time again. You describe the property you are looking for, and even if they have that exact property on their books, they will always show you at least two other properties outside of your price range and not quite right. Then, when they show you the 'real buy', it appears so much more attractive. Clever.

When managing our own finances we can be susceptible to self-imposed anchoring, and this can have damning consequences. Typically what we pay for something creates a reference of what an item is worth. At that point in time, that may be a correct assumption. It becomes dangerous when you believe that the item will always be worth this, or you won't sell something until you receive the same price you originally paid for it. Most of us accept that things change in value over time. Investments can change in value considerably. Worse, at times you can overpay for an investment, whether they are shares, a house or a business. Or you can overcapitalise, spending more on something when it doesn't necessarily increase its value.

When you let the price paid determine what you are prepared to sell something for, you are exercising a form of anchoring. This mindset can cripple you financially. For example: if you invest $50000 in the stock market and its value drops by $10000, you tell yourself, 'I will sell once it is back to $50000, so I break even.' But that can be the exact opposite of what you should do. Investing and business decisions should be based on what the investment's potential is going forward. To avoid falling into this trap you need to ask yourself, what is the value likely to do going forward? Or, knowing what you know now, would you buy it? If you wouldn't buy it as it stands, you should consider selling, even at a loss, get your money out and invest it in something that will give you a better return and make back the money that was lost.

Clients often ask me if they should sell their shares or investments. While the answer to this question can vary from client to client and stock to stock, before I can attempt to answer that question I need to take into consideration how the investment has performed so far, and how it is likely to perform. As an example, if an investment has historically underperformed over the last 15 years does this indicate that it will continue to underperform? Not necessarily. The market may have recently changed or something within the business itself may have changed for you to feel confident that the past does not indicate its potential. That said, if nothing has changed in the market and there is no new management in the company[1], then it might be fair to say that its past performance is indicative of what it is likely to keep doing. Based on that, would I keep investing in the business/company? Probably not. Would I think about cashing out? Well, that depends on what you are trying to achieve financially, but as a rule if you can get a better return elsewhere without exposing yourself to higher risk, then yes, you probably should. If you are propping up a sinking ship, then you need to walk away. Remember, with investing there are no guarantees, but you might as well increase the odds in your favour, right?

It seems straightforward, but I hear time and time again that people are not willing to sell their stock or their property until they get out what they have put in. But the odds might not be on this happening for some time, if at all. Sometimes it is better to let an investment go and find another. The fact you regret your initial decision is not an omen, it is merely a sign that it may be time to sell. Some would argue that you are realising the loss of the investment if you sell. Sure. But in not selling, the investment has still decreased in value, and the loss still exists. It's not a loss you will have to declare to the IRD, but it still exists. Believing that an unrealised loss is better than a realised loss is flawed logic and a form of denial.

If you make a rational assessment of the situation and you believe there is a real opportunity to make the loss back, and you have given yourself a timeframe to do this in, then keeping the investment may be an option. Remember though, while you are waiting for the share price to increase, you could actually be making more money elsewhere. You don't have to make money back the same way you lose it.

The extreme of anchoring is illustrated by gamblers who just want to make the money back that they have lost over the night. All this tends to result in is taking higher risks and losing more money. A less severe example might be someone who has spent $3000 fixing their $2000 car, only for the car to conk out completely the following week. If they sold the car today, they would only get $500. Yet they can't seem to shake that they had just spent $3000 the week before trying to fix it. Sure it is unfortunate, but what you spent is irrelevant and should not affect the decision of what you need to do now. Today, it is worth $500. Sell and buy another. Just don't spend more than you can afford, especially given you have just spent $3000, and then work out how you can make the $3000 back.

Spent money should no longer feature in your financial decisions. But with every investment, establish the stop-loss limit of when you will sell an asset should the investment turn pear-shaped. You must always agree on an exit strategy to realise the gain as well as a loss. It is best to agree on the exit strategy when you start.

Interestingly, the more money that's involved, the more fixated people become about not selling until they make their money back. Just because there is a lot of money involved does not change this principle. Bottom line, if you would not invest in the company today, then it is usually time to sell. That can be very hard to digest.

I had a client who had invested $1 million in a business that was slowly sinking financially. The business was unable to pay its bills (so technically insolvent, and in breach of the *Companies Act 1993*) and required an investment of $300000 to keep the doors open. Even if he invested that money it would simply prolong the pain and increase the money that he would likely never recoup. He asked me if he should do it. My answer was, it depends on what the $300000 is going to do. Is it buying the company more time, but still facing the inevitable, or is it enough to be sufficient to turn the business around? To answer this question you need to understand how the business got to where it is right now, and what, if anything, will change—other than the $300000 investment—to get a better outcome. In this instance, one of the reasons the company was in such a bad way was that it was run by incompetent directors. And they did not intend to hand over the reins to anyone else. To further complicate the matter, there was a majority shareholder who owned fifty per cent of the company, so even if we changed the board of directors she could circumvent any major decision made to turn the business around. The market conditions hadn't eased as quickly as they had hoped, nor would they any time soon.

All this brings us back to the question originally asked: whether they reinvest a further $300000 to keep this afloat. The answer was no—don't prop up a sinking ship. Take the $300000 and invest in something else that will recoup some of the loss already made. The company is worth nothing, and unless the $300000 can buy you majority shareholding and control it is throwing good money after bad. Cut your losses! Separate out the emotion and the regret and make the right decision for you now. Just because you have lost money with a certain investment does not mean that you have to earn the money back through the same investment. Sometimes letting go is the only way to move on. Just make sure that if you are making a loss, you have a strategy to make the money back. Moving on is not the same as rolling over and giving up. All this said, the clincher in my client's case was this—if he invested the $300 000 in the company his wife said she was going to leave him. Why he needed to ask me whether to invest surprised me, as the cost of investing would have been losing half of his estate, a lot more than the $300 000 discussed!

People are often reluctant to sell shares or property if they have reduced in value. While they may accept that the returns are not guaranteed, they are irrational when it comes to when to walk away. Cutting your ties and making the money up elsewhere is often the smarter move. It is important though that whenever you walk away from something, especially when you have 'lost money', that you have a clear strategy to make the money back; otherwise you may be distracted by focusing on guilt and regret.

Negative gearing

I don't know who put the positive spin on negative gearing, but they have done a great job. Negative gearing is a term used to explain when you have to 'top up' an investment, typically rental property. For every dollar you top it up by, usually you can claim up to 33 per cent back in tax. For example: If you receive rent of $300 per week, but the mortgage and rates (and other costs) come to $400 per week, you have a shortfall of $100 per week. Or, you negatively gear it by $100 per week. You get a nice juicy cheque from the IRD at the end of the year for 33 per cent of the money that you have 'topped up' the property by. And we all love to get a cheque. In a way, we probably feel that we are successfully working the system. But not really. In reality, you have paid for the tax refund, and the refund is a fraction of what you have paid. If you have the choice of having a positively geared property, with no tax refund, or a negatively geared property with a tax refund, people seem to think the negatively geared property is the winner as you are getting free money back from the IRD. This assumption is wrong.

In New Zealand it is typical for properties to be negatively geared because the rental yield tends to be low—that is, the rent you receive is often disproportionate to the value of the property and the size of the mortgage. A negatively geared property can still be a good investment, but you need to make sure that the overall capital gain over time (when the property goes up in value) outweighs the amount you have topped it up by during that same period. Sure you get money back from the IRD, but this tends to reduce the holding costs, not eliminate them altogether. So many properties go up in value, but the cost of holding them cancels out the gain, making the overall investment a waste of time.

Coupon shopping

Spending less on something you don't need or can't afford is not a smart move, irrespective of what you are saving. A deal that reduces the price of a meal, or slashes the price of accommodation, is still a big mistake if you can't afford the deal in the first place. Social marketing and discount websites seduce us with savings, which makes us overlook the key fact that we are still spending. Interestingly, when something is discounted you tend to value it less, and the redemption on discount deals is lower than if you paid full price for something. Remember, spending any amount on a 'want' when you are stressed about money or your long-term goals are being ignored is irresponsible and will likely lead to more stress. A discount is only a discount. If you can't afford it, you can't afford it. No point going bankrupt by trying to save. Just because something is a good deal does not mean you can afford it.

However, if you can afford something, getting a saving is a good thing no matter what the saving is; a dollar saved is a dollar saved. It seems that if the overall saving is a high percentage (like 50 per cent off) we are drawn like moths to the discounted flame. For example, if I find a lamp for $100 at one store, only to find the same lamp at $50 from the store across the road, I would happily cross the road to save 50 per cent. Yet when offered an opportunity to save $50 (the same amount) on a higher value purchase, like a holiday, I am happy to pass the saving up, as in the scheme of things it seems inconsequential. But a $50 saving is a $50 saving. Just because it is a small percentage of the purchanse price does not mean that it is not real money.

Short-term thinking

See it, want it, have it. Enjoy today, and expect that tomorrow will be okay. You buy something today without thinking about the impact on longer-term goals or cash flow; you buy it because you can, you have no reason not to. Often it seems like such a small amount, like a coffee or two a day. This type of thinking is easy to do when you use a credit card or you are buying something with the payment terms delayed, or the price seems inconsequential. Two cups of coffee a day only costs $10 a day, but that is $3000 per year, and over a number of years that is a trip to Europe.

Short-term thinking allows you to get the instant hit, the immediate gratification, and in a weird way to ignore the cost as it is very little today. It is usually the result of having no long-term goals, the goal being too far away or the fact that you are not seeing progression towards the goal. We tend to be programmed to think of the now, and this will continue to be the case until we have a sufficient reason not to. Which means you need to be clear about what you want, you must see progress towards that end and be motivated by it. The moment you feel that the goal is too far away, or your motivation slips, you will not bother trying. And for most of us, when we lose focus, we don't just ease back, we tend to fall off the wagon completely and undo whatever progress was made.

Worry bubbles

When you are not in control of your money you often feel disempowered to do the things you really want to, because you are worried that it simply isn't possible. You think this because you have not understood the numbers or worked out what it would take to make it happen. I often see this with people who want to do something drastic like change their career, complete a $50 000 renovation or buy a boat, but feel that their 30-year mortgage prohibits them from doing so. They create a worry bubble bigger than it needs to be. If you want to do something of consequence, or change the track you are on, you needn't compromise your longer-term goals of, say, being mortgage-free, but you will need to follow a precise financial path if you want the benefit of both worlds.

You have to be in to win

It has often been said that when possibility is in the room, probability goes out the back door. Or, when you anticipate the chance for a big gain, you downplay the odds of winning or the possible risks involved are overlooked. Lottery tickets are the best example of this. Most of us are happy to fork out $22 every week for a couple of lotto tickets because we could win, and we could win big. We don't think about the odds involved. Over the course of the year we will pay in excess of $1100. Bizarrely, many of us would be more comfortable buying a lotto ticket than banking $22 per week. Often people accept the improbable because they feel that is the only possibility of progress.

Lotto is fairly harmless because the outlay is usually slight and it gives you a bit of thrill each week with the hope of a win. But when you take the same principles and apply them to your investing decisions then you could come unstuck. Risk and return is a key concept for investing. The bigger the win offered, the more likely you could lose the money invested. Many of us never consider the risk involved and how likely we are to see the return promised, or whether we can afford to lose the money outlaid in the first place. Assess an investment in terms of what you can afford to lose without compromising your overall financial goals. If you can't afford to lose the money, you shouldn't be taking the risk, irrespective of how trustworthy the face fronting the investment is. Look behind the veneer of celebrity endorsement to the substance of the offer. It upsets me when I hear about people losing their money because of the collapse of finance companies. I expect they anticipated the promised gains and did not adequately assess the risks involved. If you don't have the skills (or an impartial adviser) to properly assess risk, then don't paddle in that pond alone.

Neurologists have found that when there is an opportunity for a big win, we are less able to make a rational assessment of risk.[2] Be aware that making this type of decision while inflamed with anticipation is unwise. Seek an impartial assessment of the deal. Remember, there is a lot of ground to cover between the anticipated gain and counting your chickens.

Research has shown that we are more afraid of the least likely things happening, and frequently not worried enough about the risks that have the greatest chance of actually occurring.[3] This means we are susceptible to being surprised about something that we should be prepared for. So often, people's financial plans assume that life is going to be sunny 365 days of the year. Even if you don't consciously believe this, a lack of savings suggests you hope it to be. We assume that we will remain employed, that the car won't blow up, we will keep getting payrises, and that the business will perform better than last year. Experience has shown this to be false. On average you are going to get two or three curve balls every year. If you have a robust plan, then you will be able to absorb these changes without compromising your momentum for the longer term. Just because these instances are infrequent does not mean that you shouldn't prepare for them. On the same note, though, you can't allow yourself to become paralysed through fear of the unknown, the unlikely, or media spin.

Holiday shopping

When you are out of your spending routine, usually because you are on holiday or to a lesser extent parental or study leave, your relationship with money tends to change, often for the worse. Holidays take us away from the daily grind and can trigger what might be abnormal behaviour. Whether it is hooking up with a stranger or being attracted to purchases that you wouldn't otherwise be drawn to, what can seem like fun in the moment can come home to roost when the credit card bill arrives. When going on holiday, set yourself a budget. I don't accept the philosophy that it's a holiday, so to hell with it. It is possible to have fun and not blow your financial future, and come home without holiday remorse.

Free lunch?

No matter how it is presented, there is no such thing as a free lunch. The very notion that the saying refers to comes from the once common practice of saloons tempting clientele into the bar with a promise of a free meal. The meal would be high in salt, encouraging them to drink more while there. In the end the extra money spent on alcohol to quench their thirst would more than pay for the lunch. It's a marketing ploy that seems to work on us time and time again. Usually, there is a real cost to something that is advertised as free. Whether it is loyalty or reward points for a credit card spend, or seductive offers (buy two, get one free), it is likely you will end up paying more overall than what you might have if no 'free' offer was advertised.

Boiled frog syndrome

When you put a frog into a pot of boiling water it will protect itself, and hop out of the pan. When you put a frog into a pot of cold water and gradually increase the temperature, it will allow itself to be boiled to death.

As it happens, our brains act much like the frog. Deep in the centre of your brain, level with the top of each ear, lie small, almond-shaped knobs of tissue called amygdalae— pronounced *ah-mig-dah-lay*. When you confront a potential risk, these parts of your reflexive brain (the emotional and intuitive part) act as an alarm system or gatekeeper to the brain—shooting signals up to the reflective brain (the thinking part) like warning flares that force the brain to react to its environment. Thanks to the amygdalae, we are more attuned to drastic changes than small incremental changes.[4] For example, the memory of a sudden drop in a financial market tends to be more disturbing than a longer, slower decline, even it if is greater overall. Managing your money and your financial future is an ongoing job. Often people's financial situation slowly deteriorates or loses momentum and they are none the wiser. Regular and impartial assessment of your financial progress will prevent a gradual decline going unnoticed.

Disturbingly, it is more common when making investing decisions to use our emotional side of the brain (the reflexive brain) to form a subconscious 'gut' assessment of an investment.[5] Here it should be the reflective brain (the analytical side of the brain) doing most of the hard work to establish whether an investment stacks up.

Peer pressure—where is the safety in numbers?

Anyone who has ever been a teenager knows that peer pressure can make you do things you might never otherwise do. It is a subtle pressure, often gradual, and its influences can be difficult to identify.

Studies have shown that when the brain is influenced by peer pressure, activity in the reflective and analytical brain is decreased. You think less about what and why, and just go with it. Logic takes a back seat when friendly influence is driving. When you go against the trend, however, the amygdalae are firing on all cylinders, creating emotional and sometimes physical pain. In short, we go along with the herd not because we have made a conscious decision to, but because it hurts not to. Where there is a large group doing something (e.g. 100 people buying today's offer), we are drawn to follow the herd instead of standing apart and making our own decision, even if it is the better one for us.

The most common money traps are:

- Burying your head in the sand

- Relinquishing control of your finances

- Investing in something for the tax benefits only

- Instant gratification or living for today

- Lack of clear medium- and long-term goals that truly motivate you

- Propping up a sinking ship

- Believing someone else will save you, or that the future will take care of itself, somehow

- Teaching your children that someone else will save them, or supporting them at your own expense

- Doing nothing

- Living in a home you can't afford, or staying at home when you need to be working

- Having more children than you can afford

- Generosity in excess of your means

- Champagne taste on a beer budget.

If you have genuinely good intentions about your money, you need to understand why you are not achieving the results you set out to. Ask yourself the following questions:

- Have I got things structured incorrectly?

- Are there obstacles outside my/our control in the way?

- Are there obstacles I/we can control that are in the way?

Some of the more frustrating cases that I have worked with were on my television show *Save Our Home*. One couple I worked with were going backwards financially and could not afford to pay their mortgage, but they would not budge on their spending. They had plenty of money coming in, but their mortgage payments were so high that they were starting to go backwards. They funded their weekly deficit with credit cards and short-term loans.

This worked for a while, until they couldn't afford the interest on the short-term borrowings. The situation had come to a climax and they were about to lose their home. They had a small window of opportunity to take ownership of the situation and overhaul their finances. But they didn't. They cussed and they cursed but did nothing. They didn't follow any of the advice given. The sad thing was that the husband seemed ready to make some concessions to move forward. But the wife was so filled with angst and frustration with the hand life had dealt her that she failed to see that she was personally contributing to their financial failure. She took no ownership for her overspending. So they continued to do nothing, even though I showed them the very simple steps they needed to take to correct their situation. In their case, they were going backwards so quickly the plan required concessions and effort, neither of which they seemed willing to make. It was an annoying outcome, as they had the power to turn things around. I believe, in the end, their house went to a mortgagee sale.

> **Tip:** If one partner does not cooperate with the joint finances, as a stop-gap, separate things out, each being responsible for certain costs, or give them a cash allowance each week. Neither of you should have carte blanche over the equity in the home. Tie up your equity, and don't let big windfalls 'catch you up'. Inheritances, payrises and bonuses should be propelling you forward—they should not be wasted on making up lost ground. However, this is only a stop-gap and won't solve the underlying niggle if you are going in different directions financially. Unless you correct this your relationship will end, or one of you will be permanently unhappy.

Overconfidence from one partner may prevent a partnership from making real progress, so call them on this.

The power of advertising

As if our personal issues aren't enough, advertising and media make it even harder to get ahead as they persuade us to buy things we probably don't need. They want us to have it, and they make us believe we need it and that we are worth it. They use common selling tricks that seem to get us every time. It is time we wised up to them all.

ROADBLOCKS TO SUCCESS

Losing weight has some simple science behind it. Eat less, exercise more. It sounds easy enough, right? For me, knowing the science doesn't make the results come any quicker or make them any easier to achieve. Given that the weight-loss industry is one of the largest and most profitable industries of our time, clearly I am not the only person who shares this experience. The same can be said for money. Getting ahead financially also has simple science behind it: spend less, repay debt faster, save. Yet, much like weight-loss, knowing what to do with your money and actually doing it are two completely different things. Knowledge does not automatically lead to action. And action does not in itself guarantee the right result.

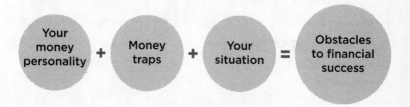

I believe that all of the most common money problems today are symptoms of whatever money traps you're in, and each symptom manifests in a different way according to your unique situation and your money personality. These factors combine to become obstacles to financial success. We need to turn these roadblocks into building blocks so you can set your sights on achieving the perfect balance.

A lot of people believe that they lack a special talent when it comes to money. But getting ahead is a skill and all skills can be learned. Like anything, some people are naturals and others have to learn the basics and practise, practise, practise. The great thing about skills is that they can be acquired and honed.

When you have run into a roadblock on the path you're following, and you can't see any alternative, it's easy to keep making the same mistakes. What makes these obstacles so tricky to overcome is that, although you may be aware of the mess you're in, it's hard to spot what you're doing wrong because you've been following the same rules for years. In fact, it has been suggested that most dysfunctional financial behaviour is learned and is 'the result of all your life experiences around money'. The good thing about this is that if the behaviour is learned, it can be unlearned.[6] The key to getting ahead is to start to recognise your feelings towards money, so you can be honest about your financial situation, and start acting smarter.

Chapter 2

Your situation

Some situations are obstacles; for example, no matter what your personality, if you are going backwards it will be impossible to get ahead until you are spending less and repaying debt. This is discussed in more detail later. There are other ingredients of your situation that may be creating barriers to your financial success.

Before you can turn things around you will need to fully understand your current situation. Think about the following things:

- What makes me happy?

- What is my financial reality?

- If you have children—what are the lessons I am teaching my kids about money?

- Do I fritter money?

- Is my debt level too high?

- Have I got a financial plan that is helping me get ahead?

- How motivated am I?

- Have I got tax problems?

- Do I have a rainy-day fund?

- If you are in a relationship—does my partner have different money values?

CAN MONEY BRING HAPPINESS?

Money is one of the many ingredients needed for happiness in the world we live in today. Materialism, or pursuing the goal of owning more stuff, is at epidemic proportions, higher than ever before. Such excess was once reserved for nobility, but is now more widely experienced by the masses—this is illustrated by the fact it is the masses to which most advertising campaigns are targeted. The problem with materialism is that it becomes a treadmill and can prioritise itself higher than it should. It leads to getting a bigger house or better car, going on holiday to Europe and spending a small fortune on incidentals each week. The benefits of this spending are celebrated, but the costs are seldom acknowledged and can extend beyond the financial. For example, the result of spending more and more is that you need to use credit, or other people's money (usually the bank's). This results in higher credit card balances. Because you want the bigger, better house, your mortgage payments increase over time, rather than reducing. This can lead to a stay-at-home spouse needing to return to work, work overtime or take a second job, or, worse yet, having to work beyond retirement age. The often ignored, or at best undiscussed, impact of these decisions is less time with family, friends and yourself. This is sure to have a cost beyond the dollar spent.

Which then brings us to the next question—are we even happier with such choices? Research suggests that the extra debt we incur to get the bigger homes and better cars does not even make us happier. In fact, the opposite is true— more materialistic people are less happy, and have poorer psychological health and emotional wellbeing, than those who are less materialistic.[7] That does not mean all financial goals are psychologically unhealthy. Nor does it mean that you shouldn't live in a nice house and drive a nice car. If you can do that *and* be happy, then you have found the perfect balance.

All goals are not created equal in their happiness-producing effect. Pursuit of the wrong goals will not make you happy if the goal itself is out of alignment with your core values. That said, it has been proven that positive and functional financial goals contribute to happiness. Whether that goal is being mortgage-free or saving for your children's education, a wedding or your retirement will be a personal decision, but these are all examples of positive financial goals. Research has shown that these goals all correlate with better wellbeing.[8]

But can money bring you happiness? Money helps you put food on the table and enjoy a nice cup of coffee at the local cafe. Money helps you educate your children, to better their opportunities, and that has got to feel good. Money can buy you health care and a nice house in a nice neighbourhood. It can allow you to go on holidays and be generous with friends. In short, money can help you get other things that make you happy. So is it the only way to find happiness? If you have overspent, then probably not—lasting happiness has to be free of anxiety and stress. I have found, with my own family and many of my clients, that money can only bring happiness to a point—as the popular song says, for every ten rich men there is only one with a satisfied mind. Money spent beyond that point does not make you incrementally happier.

The money spent that doesn't bring happiness is the money that gets frittered. And for most of us, the frittered money—the bit that slips through our fingers without being accounted for—is usually the money that we cannot afford to spend. The money–happiness connection is dictated by the law of diminishing returns. The more you spend, the less satisfaction you derive from each additional dollar spent.

The law of diminishing returns is one of the most famous laws in all of economics and it plays a central role in production theory. The basic definition is that in a productive process, if you keep adding one more unit of something while holding all other components constant, at some point the unit added will produce less. To illustrate this concept using economics, you may say that watering a garden produces a better flower. And the more you water it the better the quality of flower, to a point. Beyond the point of optimal water consumption, you could keep watering the plants but they will not produce better quality produce because at some point the plants will become saturated. On a personal basis, you may love movies and enjoy watching a lot of them. But if you watched too many, you would hit saturation point. Spending money also has a saturation point for happiness and I believe this plays a central role in managing money, too. The money spent beyond the happiness threshold is money frittered and, generally, it's money that could be saved or put towards debt repayment leaving you just as happy or happier.

If you can find the money beyond your happiness threshold that is being frittered then you have found the easiest way to get ahead—stop frittering it. If you received no lasting satisfaction from a purchase, not making similar purchases in the future should not reduce your happiness. Chances are, your happiness will increase without making these purchases because guilt is the easiest way to offset any happiness—and it's the quickest way to kill any purchasing buzz. Note, though, that additional complexities can arise with couples, as we each tend to have different happiness thresholds. The differences have to be recognised and respected, otherwise the benefit from improving your financial future may be offset by divorce proceedings.

Applying this principle, the most sustainable way of getting ahead or spending less money is to find the 'frittered money', the money spent beyond the point of your money–happiness threshold. That's the spending that does not bring you any additional satisfaction. To be sustainable, it is important that you don't compromise your general satisfaction. This refinement process takes time. With some clients it can take up to twelve months to get there. As situations change, so do the triggers for happiness. The process involves projections, tracking results and making refinements. It involves getting reconnected with what brings you happiness compared to how much it costs, compared to where it leaves you financially speaking. For me, this money triangle is the crux of the problem and recognising this is the key to lasting success.

Few people actually know what they are spending. Fewer people know what they could stop spending without affecting their level of happiness.

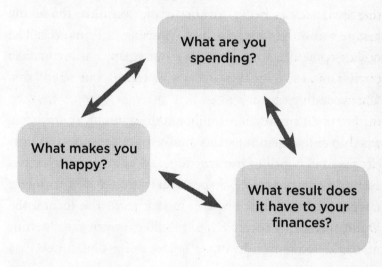

YOUR FINANCIAL REALITY

Everybody has things they enjoy, things that are important to them and things they like to do. Probably, they secretly feel a sense of entitlement to do these things. Whether frivolous or not, you need to recognise what your 'wants' cost. Consider whether you want something because you have always had it, or does it truly make you happy? It is not until you start to go through the process of elimination that you can rule out needs versus wants. And it is important if you are going to make any form of concession in any area that you are able to feel the immediate financial benefit of your actions, otherwise you will lose motivation faster than you thought possible.

How is it that you can get a payrise, a legitimate and tangible increase in income, yet you do not feel the difference? Or, having made a concerted effort to spend less in one area, you do not feel any better off overall, as the saving just gets absorbed into the black hole of your finances. The money comes in, and it goes back out again. These common complaints are indications that you are disconnected from your spending.

Frittered money is usually small amounts spent often that do not contribute to your lasting happiness. Many people may consider my morning cup of coffee a frivolous expense, that the money I spend on it is wasted or frittered. I have always purchased this coffee from the local cafe. Do I need to buy coffee? Could I make it from the machine at work? Do I need to buy a coffee every day? In exploring these questions I found that my morning coffee is a non-negotiable cost. It's frivolous, it's cheap, but it is still a non-negotiable to me as I am definitely happier having had a decent cup of coffee every morning. By definition, therefore, the money I spend on it is not frittered. However, on average, I have found that people fritter 10–15 per cent of their income. This is money they spend because they can, because they have no reason not to, or because they are doing what they have always done and don't even realise they are doing it. Remember what is frittered spending for one person may be a non-negotiable cost to another. When assessing whether your costs are non-negotiable or not be open-minded, as in my experience people are surprised when they learn what makes them happy and what costs, when not incurred, have little effect to their overall wellbeing.

I specialise in helping my clients find the money they are frittering. When this is executed effectively they can save while continuing to live the lifestyle they enjoy, and the overwhelming feedback is 'I don't even feel like I am on a budget.' You too need to look at your expenses and determine which are giving you real happiness, and which purchases you might be prepared to spend less, or willing to go without if the money you save can contribute to your long-term happiness.

> **Money does, and always will, matter.**

CHILDREN AND MONEY

For many of us, a common reason why we don't make the progress we might otherwise make is that we have children. It's natural for parents to happily go without in order to give to their children or grandchildren. As a parent myself, I relate to parents' desire to give everything they possibly can to their children. Often, this is to give them the opportunities we never had, and to enjoy the efforts of our hard work. Too often, though, it is to give them too much. Sadly, this can rob children of experiencing the joy of success, of having worked for achievement.

One of the sweetest feelings comes from enjoying the fruits of your own labour. If you rob your kids of this, you deprive them of the satisfaction and joy hard work brings and they don't learn the much-needed life skill of delaying gratification. Most importantly, you may even be setting them up for financial failure. A child needs to learn the value of a dollar. They need to understand that when the money runs out, there is no money. They need to understand how the money comes in and where it goes. To understand how they contribute and take from the family finances they need to be connected to the family and the family's financial woes and successes. This is life, and if you are a parent part of your job is to help your children connect with, and remain connected to, their financial reality.

In sheltering your children from the financial reality of your situation, which is often theirs as well, you are enabling financial ineptitude. If things are tight at home, the best action you can take is to sit your children down to explain things and agree as a family how you are going to get the situation back on track. If you do not take the time to do this, your children will see that it is okay to overspend, as there are never any consequences. This is equally true for adult children. Parents may have a genuine belief that they are helping their children, but if you are continuing to pay for costs when your children are working, even part time, how can you expect them to understand what it costs to live and to take responsibility for their own financial decisions? Too often I see parents charging their adult children board at a fraction of what it is costing to run the house. Their response is they are not comfortable charging more. While I'm not encouraging you to make money off your children's board, you need to be realistic about the costs.

Spending money you don't have, even if it's on your children, helps no-one. If anything it creates an expectation on the child's behalf that you will bail them out or continue to contribute to an activity even if you cannot afford it. As a parent you are always going to want to give as much as you can to children, but your generosity must not compromise your own financial stability, otherwise no-one wins. This is especially important for single parents or a single-income household.

As parents you have a duty to arm your children financially. Children tend to have high activity costs and this is accepted as a non-negotiable expense. While components of their activities may in fact be non-negotiable, don't create an expectation that you can sustain something when you can't, and communicate when you have used up all available funds. Otherwise, all that happens is children will find more activities with more costs, and you will be left feeling forced to continue in the vein in which you started. A child gifted in sports or academia can often be a financial curse.

It's easy to buy into the notion that you can afford to ignore the financial impact of your decisions if it is for a 'greater cause' (children, religion, friends, a good time). However, you need to be able to see when your children are genuinely in need of assistance, as opposed to needing a bailout. If your adult child is working full time then they shouldn't need assistance. If they do, it usually indicates they are spending more than they earn. You giving them money, or facilitating their lifestyle, may become habitual and dangerous for both of you. A family working together so that everyone can get ahead faster is different. For example, parents who provide equity in their own home as a means for their children to purchase their first home can be a good way to truly help your children, and yourself.

You do not want to foster the expectation that someone will save them. 'Someone else will save me' is the belief that you don't have to manage your money because someone or something is going to gallop to the rescue any minute now. Parents continually gallop to their children's aid, usually on a debt-laden horse and often to their kids' detriment.

Pocket money

If you don't have financial troubles, then set your children up for success. Show them how to budget successfully. Their money personalities will start to emerge when they are young, so you need to equip them with the skills to work around natural tendencies, where necessary.

Pay pocket money in exchange for work done. Even if the work is as simple as keeping their room tidy, ensure they do this before paying the pocket money. It is all too common for teenage children to want to spend more than they have been given and then come and ask for more money. If you then encourage overspending by giving them more money, you have given a signal that overspending is okay. What skill does that teach them? I don't know of any instances where overspending hasn't come back to bite the spender. Yet during your children's formative learning, it's very easy to teach them that it is okay to spend and not worry about tomorrow. This is a very effective way of derailing your plan for your children to have a better life than yours.

Teach your children the right skills. I encourage my clients to bring all their family to our meetings. I do this because families have goals, and in working through every-day financial issues together every member of a family is learning. If you can't manage your money properly, how do you expect your children to learn? They won't learn financial literacy at school. They won't learn it at university. They need to learn about financial literacy from you and your mistakes, otherwise they will have to learn from their own mistakes. If the perfect balance eludes you, how can you possibly show your children how to find it?

> **Let your mistakes be the making of your children.**

Teach them that money does, and always will, matter. Teach them they are to use money to find the perfect balance of living the life they want and getting ahead financially. Money is supposed to be controlled; it is not supposed to control you. The unfortunate thing about money is that if you stuff things up too often, it is very hard to correct things. Pocket money is a good place to start. Here is my simple guide for pocket money and where and how to start discussing money with your children.

From the age of four, give children $1 for every year of their age. Pay the pocket money with one-dollar coins—five one-dollar coins for a five-year-old and ten one-dollar coins for a ten-year-old.

When you start paying pocket money, sit down together with the coins and go through a budget allocating the money as follows:

- 20 per cent to a charity of the child's choosing

- 20 per cent to savings

- 60 per cent to spend now—for living costs and entertainment.

For a ten-year-old that means:

- $2 for charity

- $2 into the piggy bank

- $6 for spending now.

This process teaches children some important lessons. First, money is real—it is tangible. You can see it and feel it and it runs out. Children are often introduced to money through Mum's wallet or eftpos card. If it is not Mum's, it's Dad's. The problem with eftpos cards is that they are magical. There always seems to be money available, and if there isn't, the credit card is always there for back-up. If you know how much money you have to spend, and you know that money runs out, you learn to make smarter decisions as each dollar has to count for something. You quickly become connected to what you need to spend to create happiness. Note also that when your child has spent all their money and they want more, you should tell them to wait until their next pocket-money payday, or do more jobs to get more money sooner.

For the 20 per cent allocated to charities, it is important your child can identify with the charity. Research charities together to find one they want to help, and make an effort to hand deliver the money once it has accumulated. It is good to give first and think of others. As they select a charity to support they will think about what makes them feel good. Giving to others is not reserved for Christians. It is an effective way of increasing self-esteem and has psychological benefits. One weakness of the modern world is that most things are virtual. You miss out on the tactility of decisions. So if they decide to donate to the SPCA, make sure you visit the nearest SPCA centre so they can see physically what they are helping.

Don't judge your children's choice of charity, or try to coerce them towards your preference—it's about learning to give. The busker outside of my local supermarket has benefited from my three-year-old's charity on more than one occasion.

Saving for the future is about setting a goal and working towards it. Start them thinking about something they might want. Suggest they find a picture of the desired object and put it on the fridge. Let them go through the process of saving for something. Let them earn the satisfaction that comes for saving for something and getting what they want. If you want to encourage them to save for a big-ticket item; for example, a state-of-the-art mountain bike, you might offer to match their savings dollar for dollar.

With the spending money, encourage them to live for now and if there's money left over at the end of the week, encourage them to put it in the piggy bank.

BEING SELF-EMPLOYED

Most self-employed people become so because they want the chance to be their own boss, to work the hours they want and to earn the money they want. In reality, they tend to work harder than ever and make less money than before. They are never able to leave work behind as it follows them through their weekends and into the following weeks. They never really have a day off because they are conscious, more than ever before, that the money might run out. You make hay while the sun shines—if the sun keeps shining of course you are going to keep making hay. Yet, for all that effort, it seems hard to find the balance—for many it's a constant struggle.

One of the common issues with being self-employed is a tendency to morph everything into one. Unfortunately most self-employed people tend to intermingle their personal affairs with the business, with the idea that it will allow them to push some personal costs into the business and claim a tax deduction. While I am all for maximising your tax efficiencies, doing it this way is often counterproductive, with a possible tax saving being offset by the fact that the money shouldn't have been spent in the first place, or you have created a general haze over how well the business is in fact performing. Also, if you aren't careful and don't keep good records of your spending, this might result in a tax return showing shareholder salaries or drawings as an amount greater than what was paid to you in cash from the business.

Another curse of being self-employed is that people are prepared to spend more or buy things that they might not have bought through their business simply because it is tax deductible. Yes, in New Zealand, for every dollar you spend you will get a 28 cent deduction—an offset in tax that you would otherwise have to pay. However, if money is tight and you are buying something you don't really need this is a false economy—it's not the right thing to be doing. I once had a client who took me out for lunch and said don't worry, 'it's tax deductible.' My reply was yes, but for every dollar you are spending, you are only saving yourself 28 cents. So in most instances, wouldn't you be better not spending the dollar? It is easy to push costs through your business. But if you are not going to be better off financially for the cost incurred, it is still a waste.

This is often the same for people who have a mortgage on an investment property. They love getting tax deductions on the property but they are physically paying for the tax deduction and the deduction is a fraction of what they paid. (See the section on negative gearing above.) For example, people often tell me that they would never pay off the mortgage on their investment property, even if they have no other mortgage to repay. They say they get heaps of tax benefits from the property, which is usually true. But if you received a tax rebate or a deduction against your salary, of say $1500 per annum, you have actually paid $4500 in real cash to qualify for that refund. So if you have an opportunity to reduce your tax loss by repaying the principal faster, which in turn reduces the interest cost—makes the property cost less—you need to take this opportunity. Because in repaying the mortgage you save $1 in interest costs and forfeit 33 cents of tax refund.

Overall, you are 67 cents better off—and that 67 cents is cash in the back pocket.

Being paid in cash is often hailed as one of the many benefits of being self-employed, as you don't need to pay tax on the money received. Technically you are supposed to declare cash received as income to the IRD, but if there is no paper trail your accountant is never going to know, and neither will the IRD, right? Yep. The problem with cash is that it is more likely to feel like 'free money' than earned money. It feels like a windfall, so you treat it like a windfall—that is, with little regard. You end up spending the money on stuff. Wasted stuff. So on the one hand you could pay tax on the $1 cash, and pocket 70 cents. You lose 30 cents but psychologically your attitude towards the money changes. The money becomes part of your finances, not sitting attractively to one side, seducing you with temptation. Alternatively, you might keep it out of the finances, keep 100 per cent of it, but waste the entire lot.

I had one client who was self-employed and pocketed $150 000 in cash every year. He doesn't declare this as income to the IRD. I asked him where the money was. The answer was nowhere—it is spent. On what? I asked. The money went on holidays, cars, clothes, shoes and entertainment, all discretionary items, no necessities. Fancy that, $150 000 per year. I asked him if spending this level of money on discretionary stuff was necessary for his happiness. He thought probably not.

Being paid in cash doesn't need to be a bad thing, but if the cash is more readily spent, then it is. One way to get around this is to compare what you have received in cash versus what you would have received if you had been paid normally, after tax. If there is a positive difference, put that to one side and spend away. But the rest needs to go towards standard living costs, otherwise you are going to be worse off from being paid cash.

Another problem with being self-employed is that, because income is irregular, budgeting can seem pointless. Without a budget you will have little control over your financial future. When money comes in, you can live like a king—you have a feast-or-famine existence that results in little to no progress being made overall.

Here are my top tips for the self-employed:

- Always pay yourself in cash, not in kind.

- Always charge in cash, not in kind.

- Stop putting personal costs through the business.

- If your business shows a profit, you should be able to take that money in cash.

- Reduce your debtors.

- Even out your income over time.

- Pay tax on what you owe—there is no point in making an enemy out of the IRD.

- Consider paying tax monthly, based on monthly profit, to avoid big provisional tax bills.

- Get help to run your business better.

- If you have to, get a new accountant.

Most people who are self-employed excel at the service they provide or product they produce. This is their strength. Running a business or making money is not. If this is you, you need to seek good business advice to avoid poor historical performance dictating future business potential. All my clients know that I do not accept poor business performance. That being said, highlighting a problem and fixing said problem are not the same thing. If my clients are ready to get some different results I will show them what needs to happen to turn things around. The crux of this, though, is whether they are prepared to do things differently. It's easy to talk about changing your ways, but talking and doing are not one and the same.

Without bagging accountants—after all, I am one—if your accountant is not sitting down regularly to help you plan ahead, then I would suggest you change accountants. All too often, accountants simply tell you what you have done when you actually need to know what you need to do next.

Chapter 3

Financial literacy

Our lives today are fuller than ever. We work longer hours and commute further to work in heavier traffic. The cost of living keeps increasing faster than salaries can respond. House prices get higher and higher, almost irrationally. Yet our response to our busier lives and higher costs is not to spend less. Instead we are the highest consumers of recent generations, living bigger and better than ever before. Houses are bigger and cars are better, and most families have two. Designer clothes and overseas travel are no longer reserved for the rich, and we all have the latest electronics—iPhones, flat screen TVs and iPads. What once was considered extravagance is now standard.

But these living costs come at a high price and, for many, are financed by debt, or credit. Debt was once discouraged, to be used only in exceptional circumstances, and was not so readily available, yet it now seems to be the rule. Surveys have suggested that we lack basic financial knowledge about how to successfully manage this debt—well you don't say! What is interesting, though, is that research suggests that the extra debt we incur to get the bigger homes and better cars—the supposed better life—does not make us happier. More materialistic people are less happy, and have poorer psychological health and emotional wellbeing than those who are less materialistic.[9] I am not suggesting that all financial goals are, in themselves, psychologically unhealthy. Some, in fact, are quite the opposite and have been shown to contribute to happiness. Positive and functional goals, like saving for the deposit on your first home, saving for your kid's university studies or your retirement, correlate with better psychological health. Research has further suggested that materialistic goals, or objectives that are realised through borrowing instead of saving, do not improve your psychological health, and can in fact decrease your psychological wellness.[10]

Many households are unfamiliar with even the most basic economic concepts needed to make sensible saving and investment decisions. We have unprecedented numbers of households arriving at retirement with little to no savings or wealth. Both the young and old are woefully under-informed about financial concepts as they relate to savings, retirement, mortgages and other decisions. This lack of knowledge will become more of an issue as benefits and pensions decline. This means it is becoming more important for people to acquire economic know-how and understand the tricks of the trade. As you improve your financial understanding of products and concepts, your financial wellbeing improves. Remember, no-one cares about your money as much as you.

Disconcertingly, a survey conducted by ANZ Banking Group suggested that when financial knowledge is weak, people tend to be more confident about their abilities than warranted. It is not a new concept for the ignorant to be arrogant. What is disappointing though is that New Zealand has one of the highest levels of financial ignorance in the developed world. Yet our misplaced confidence seems to be a deterrent to seeking professional advice (not helped by the quality of some the supposed 'professionals'), thereby widening the knowledge gap.

The same ANZ survey found that 80 per cent of respondents were confident about their understanding of financial issues, but only half of those people answered at least 50 per cent of the questions correctly when given questions to answer and problems to solve about those issues.[11]

If you are feeling overwhelmed by money then at least you know that you need help and could do it better. The study above suggests that 80 per cent of the people who do need help don't know it, or choose not to believe it. Remember, it's never too late to learn the concepts of getting ahead faster and, taking away the jargon, the 'how to' is easy to understand. You just have to learn the rules of money.

> Remember, it is never too late to change your financial landscape.

THE RULES OF MONEY

Money's role in society has not changed in thousands of years. It is how our success (at least on earth) is measured. For those who understand the rules of money, or the tricks of the trade, it becomes a game that you are able to play to win.

Among other things, learning these laws will increase your financial literacy, helping you to become a financially responsible citizen. Hopefully if you have children you will teach them the rules so they, too, become responsible citizens. Unless you know what you have to know, you cannot be expected to do what you need to do and nor can your children.

The same three rules of money apply to everyone, no matter how old they are, or how much they earn:

- Rule one: It's not how much you make, but how much you keep

- Rule two: Cash is king

- Rule three: Progress is queen.

IT'S NOT HOW MUCH YOU MAKE, BUT HOW MUCH YOU KEEP

Income levels do not indicate how fast you can get ahead. Never think that you need to earn more to make progress. You may need to alter your tastes, but you should be able to live comfortably on what you are currently earning. In fact, often for those on higher incomes the income itself acts as a deterrent to real progress. A high income usually provides a sense of security that for many is psychological rather than real. More often than not the higher income is not spent increasing one's wealth—it is just spent. For example, it's not uncommon to receive a payrise but not feel any better off financially. The extra income is just absorbed by day-to-day living costs instead of propelling you forward. The more money you earn, the less you worry about your financial future, but this lack of concern is usually not warranted.

To get ahead financially—not to sink slower, not to float or merely fly, but to fly to your destination faster—you need to have money left over at the end of each week. If you do not have money left over, or if you have to use a credit card to fund your lifestyle, you are likely going backwards financially. Everyone needs to spend less than they earn. Until you master this one fact, you have little chance of achieving the perfect balance. You can dress yourself up as much as you want, hanging your hat on being asset-rich or earning a good salary, but the first step to real progress is to have money left over so that you can see your savings grow.

> Question: How much should you have left over at the end of each week?
> Answer: A minimum of 10 per cent of your earnings.

If you earn $100 per week, you need to have at least $10 left over—sitting in a bank account—at the end of each week. The money is either left over or it is not—if you cannot see 10 per cent of your weekly income sitting in your bank account you have not mastered the first step.

If you are having trouble nailing this first step, it's not because there is a secret formula that only an accountant can understand. It is because you are spending too much. But don't feel like you are struggling alone. Benjamin Franklin once said, 'If you know how to spend less than you get, you have the philosopher's stone.'

For most of us, having money left over does not come naturally. But there are things you can do to make it easier.

First, before you spend, you must always make sure you 'future proof first'. That is, put aside 10 per cent of your net earnings, irrespective of your income level. This means earmarking the money you are saving for the future. Some financial advisers describe this as paying yourself first, but I find this description misleading. 'Paying yourself' is often misinterpreted as spending on yourself first. But self-spending should never be the first thing you do.

Unfortunately, while tithing to your church or giving to a charity may be a worthwhile thing to do, it does not guarantee a successful financial outcome for you and does not offset any of your savings obligations or the need to future-proof financially.

Stop living for now—there are some serious financial issues looming, which my generation and our children are going to face. These issues are being ignored by many people and even governments around the world.

You need to be on your game before things go bad. Pay yourself first—put aside money for the future. Make sensible investments and reduce your debt; for example, pay off your mortgage faster. (See 'Getting rid of your mortgage' on page 128 for more on this subject.)

These savings, for many, start from insignificant beginnings. Most do not kickstart their wealth creation or saving regime with a bang. Many of us are not fortunate enough to receive a financial windfall, or a cash injection from parents wanting to lend a helping hand. Thankfully, financial success does not restrict itself to how much you start with. Wealth does not favour people, or align itself with the rich, but it does favour process. Like a tree, wealth often grows from a tiny seedling. Some are lucky enough to circumvent the seedling stage, and their wealth is propagated (usually by their parents) as a small plant. That said, the strength and size of a tree has nothing to do with the size of the seed, but rather how the seed is indulged. For most of us, the first dollar you save is like the seedling. If you diligently attend to it, protecting it from the winds of temptation, nourishing it with interest earnings and fertilising it with more savings, it will continue to grow. Consistency in all weather conditions is the key to creating your wealth tree. The sooner you plant the seed, the sooner you will see it grow.

Most people have saved in their life from time to time. Many have successfully saved for a clear goal; for example, their first car, or the big OE. Few, however, are able to save consistently and diligently. Saving is not a noun, it is a verb—it is in the doing that you get results.

With the remaining 90 per cent of your income, work out how to live a lifestyle you can enjoy. If you are using credit cards to supplement your lifestyle then you can't afford your current way of life—you are living beyond your means and will be going backwards, even if it doesn't feel like it yet. Champagne taste on a beer budget is a recipe for financial disaster.

> **Question: How do you know that you can afford your lifestyle?**
> **Answer: You can pay with cash.**

With the money you spend, enjoy life. It's important not to overspend, but it is also important that you don't try to save too much. If 10 per cent is all you can comfortably keep for your savings, then let it be. How can you save 10 per cent of your income when 90 per cent is insufficient to cover your necessary expenditure? Good question. What I have learned is that people's 'necessary' expenses always increase as they earn more. You always spend to your income. My personal situation is testament to this. When we graduated from university my husband and I had a combined income of $32,000 per annum. I thought I was the richest person in the world— let's face it, any income is better than being a student. Eight years and many payrises later I was earning more than ever, but was left asking where all the money had gone. Sure, I had a couple of properties, but it felt like I had just created a big treadmill that I needed to keep turning, and it was tiring.

It is common to be running hard, but going nowhere. I have many clients that earn more than $500000 per annum, but they are spending most of this on their lifestyle. There is no money left at the end of the month. Sure, they are living well, but it's from payday to payday.

Question: How can you live on 90 per cent of your income when 90 per cent is not enough?
Answer: You just have to!

The key is not to confuse your desires with necessary expenditure. Choose the things that are important to you, even if they seem frivolous, and make sure you have money to spend on these things. Not everything is important, so choose carefully. For example, my non-negotiable costs include having a hot chocolate each day from a favourite cafe, having a cleaner, brunch with my family on the weekend and swimming lessons for my son. I do not bother defending these. Because they are important to me I have to factor it into my budget.

Think about all the money you spend and distinguish between desires and needs. Remember when you received your first pay check—it went a long way. You were earning less, spending less, but were just as happy (I presume). Some frivolity is needed, but think carefully. If all your desired spending cannot be incorporated into the 90 per cent of your income allocated for spending, recognise that you must let some desires go unsatisfied and move on. Keep adjusting your budget.

Consider what you really want—nice clothes, a bit of finery, more coffees? Or do you want more substantial assets, the opportunity to work less, to be mortgage-free or to buy a family bach? Do you want to have a retirement you can enjoy? The 90 per cent you spend covers the basics, the 10 per cent you save brings the future you want.

If you find living on 90 per cent of your income impossible you need to understand the psychology of your spending. What obstacles are in the way? If you think your natural tendencies may be the main reason why you are not able to do this, then you need to change the way you do things or get expert help. But do something—it is your financial and social responsibility to do something.

Debt should only be used to acquire more assets. An

asset is something that goes up in value over time. Consumer goods, as a rule, do not increase in value—they depreciate. So if you need to use debt to cover your day-to-day living costs—as opposed to investing—again, you can dress it up however you want, but you are going backwards.

You need to stop right now and appreciate each dollar spent and be happier for it. Link your spending to your happiness. I accept that you need money to be happy, to a point. But spending beyond that point does not make you incrementally happier for every extra dollar you spend. Most of us could spend less and be just as happy. We usually spend because we can, not because we have to. I spend hours going through this process with my clients as we start the journey to understand what needs to be spent and link it to their overall satisfaction. If you find it too hard to stop— often a sign that you are too far on the back foot, with your debts too high—and you find that too much money is going into servicing your debt, you will not make progress.

Remember the first thing you ever purchased and how you saved hard for it . . . and when you got it, how amazing you felt. The first thing I remember saving for was a pair of Reebok running shoes, white with purple stitching—very chic. My husband first saved for a Sony Walkman.

When you saved and acquired this special item, it meant something—you enjoyed it, you flaunted it and it made you happy, pure and true. Then you grew up, earned heaps of money, bought lots of stuff, but with each new purchase the satisfaction lasted less and less. This has to be changed.

I think everyone has two to three things that are important to them that they should be able to identify as non-negotiable deal breakers. Work out what these are for you and look for ways to reduce spending on everything else. To help you identify areas of spending that you may be able to cut, the most common areas of these casual wants can be categorised by gender as follows:

- Women like good coffee, a glass of wine now and then, holidays, socialising with friends, and buying presents for friends and family.

- Men like buying toys, family holidays, alcohol and sports.

Once you have worked out what you need and what you want, draw up a budget, remembering the best budgets create a feeling of consciousness around your spending but do not leave you feeling deprived. If you are having trouble finding this balance, you need to get assistance.

> **A budget is supposed to enable you to achieve your desires—it is not supposed to restrict you.**

A Roman philosopher once said that 'Luck is what happens when preparation meets opportunity.' George S. Clason says, 'Opportunity is a haughty goddess who wastes no time with those who are unprepared.' If you want to start getting ahead, get organised. Opportunity tends to run in organisation's shadow.

THE 10 PER CENT SAVED

Get the 10 per cent saved working for you—it's just the start. If you can get it to grow or, better still, multiply, you will start to pick up momentum towards financial success. The easiest way to grow the funds is to invest them wisely. If invested wisely they will increase quickly.

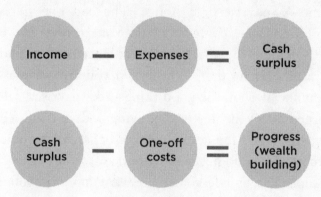

Warning: Do not get misled by a romantic desire to make wealth too quickly. The first principle of investment is guaranteeing your investment. Do not be tempted by larger earnings or bigger returns if there is a chance you can lose your investment. Make sure you can get access to your funds if you need to. Remember the penalty of risk is probable loss. You have worked hard for that 10 per cent—do not lose it by being impatient.

The cash surplus can be used to cover your one-off costs. Many people can successfully live within their means on a day-to-day basis, but when one-off costs happen—for example, going on holiday, buying a car, or visiting the dentist—their cash surplus is insufficient to cover these costs. No-one can afford to wipe out their daily progress with one-off costs—it is not sustainable. You need to be allowing for these costs as part of your budget, otherwise you will find that life's curve balls will limit or stop your progress.

Most of us get two or three curve balls every year and some are good, some bad. The good ones increase your income—a payrise or a bonus. The bad ones increase your costs—your car conks out, your roof starts leaking. Over time the good tend to balance out the bad, or they negate each other. However, if you are not working to a financial plan, the good things, like payrises, will be absorbed into your day-to-day living and you will feel no better for it. Yet the negative curve balls will become the reason why you do not make progress.

Remember, it is common to want more as you earn more and it is universal to want more than you can afford. (Champagne taste on a beer budget is not a new phenomenon.) Classical economics suggests it is human nature to want more. Sociologists and anthropologists suggest our personal tastes and personalities explain only a small part of why we buy. All exchange, from gifts to barter to purchases, is social. We love to emulate others, or at least attempt emulation. People generally behave in ways that are rewarded and avoid doing what is punished in their societies.

Advertising and media fan the fire of our desires, giving us permission to buy now even if we can't afford it. We are encouraged to be discontented with what we have and want better for our family and ourselves. We live in a never-ending cycle of seeing, wanting, buying—with or without ready cash—then having to work more to pay for it. To run faster on our own financial treadmills. The more you have the more you want, and this is a symptom of the socially transmitted and advertising-encouraged disease of 'affluenza'. Affluenza has been defined by Oliver James, a British psychologist, as a spending epidemic, resulting from the never-ending pursuit of more and 'keeping up with the Joneses'. Affluenza is obsessive in nature, results in debt overload and has led to huge increases in anxiety and depression in the Western world.[12] It's thought the economic growth of the Western world is based on organised dissatisfaction of the masses. The only antidote to affluenza I've found is saving 10 per cent of your income and living your life with the rest. Don't bother keeping up with the Joneses if the Joneses are broke.

Planning and controlling how much you consume are key components underlying wealth building. Most people give little time to preparing or planning for their financial future. In fact, they are more likely to spend more time planning a holiday than planning for their retirement. But you have to take time to plan your budget. If you don't have time to do this, outsource it to someone else, but make sure you are working to a plan. Operating a household without a budget is like running a business without a plan, without goals, without direction.

If you are spending more than you earn and you are not successfully managing to change this, you need to enlist expert help to kickstart your progress.

TIPS FOR SAVING MONEY

There are many ways that you can save money on living costs—in most instances you simply need to be more organised. Here are my top tips for saving. Each of these changes, in isolation, can translate to little financial gain, but when combined you can save thousands of dollars each year.

Use cash

Although credit cards are a convenient source of money, if they are not repaid on time they can easily become a drag on your income, eroding your cash flow and costing you in extra interest. In addition, credit cards encourage spending—most people are willing to spend more when they use a credit card than when using cash. Studies have shown that less transparent forms of payment tend to be treated like 'play money' and are, therefore, more easily used. Cash is viewed as the most transparent form of payment[13], so always use cash if you can and structure your finances accordingly.

For practical reasons you may wish to keep one credit card and limit its use to occasional purchases when other methods of payment are not appropriate; for example, internet purchases. To avoid problems, it may be helpful to run your credit card with a positive balance so that reaching a zero balance will serve as a mental check to further spending. All other cards should be cut up. And remember that being able to pay your credit card in full each month does not mean that you couldn't spend less.

Work cost reimbursement

Have a separate credit card to pay for costs that will be reimbursed by your work, so that you know it is outside of your plan and will be taken care of separately. People often pay for work-related things—taxis or lunches—with their eftpos or credit card. Although the money will eventually be reimbursed, the delay in repayments puts unnecessary pressure on personal finances until it is reimbursed. There is also a risk that you forget to claim the expense, or not do it on a timely basis. I recommend you have a separate credit card for these types of situations. You only use it if you are incurring costs for others that you know will be reimbursed later. It keeps things clean, minimises unclaimed costs and avoids any costs or delays in reimbursement straining your personal finances.

Keep business and personal finance separate

Many self-employed people run their businesses as an extension of their personal finances, or vice versa. Every-thing tends to be intertwined, which just means things are a mess. Financial statements are usually manipulated to ensure profit is low, so the tax to pay is low, with little regard for how much money the business is actually earn-ing and spending. If it is common to be short of money in the business, people may willingly top it up from their personal finances, or not pay themselves a salary to ensure the business' sustainability. Some business costs are paid from personal accounts or by credit card, and some busi-ness owners and self-employed people are more comfortable spending because they believe the cost is tax deductible. Any combination of these points usually ensures that you are not taking from the business what you could and should.

Very few small businesses actually forecast earnings, instead reacting only to provisional tax payments. Forecasting income and the timing of expenses is key. Too often business owners confuse possible with probable in the sense that they back themselves with the 'bigger-picture, broad-brush, she'll be right' attitude and are less concerned with the nuts and bolts of how to get a positive outcome. While an entrepreneurial attitude is critical to self-employment, 80 per cent of businesses fail with most small-to-medium businesses failing to unlock their true capabilities. Forecasting and accountability to the financial implications of every decision is key. However, when it is your business, emotion and an owner's willingness to keep injecting cash, or forfeiting a shareholder salary, work against sound business principles. Tracking to a sustainable and achievable business plan is key. Business strategy is imperative if you are going to grow your business the smartest way. If you do not know how to do this, get advice.

Another key benefit of keeping everything separate is that it will highlight actual business performance and whether the business in its current state is viable. Not all good ideas translate to good businesses or financial gains. And not all good operators have a viable product or service. A good idea, in isolation, means zilch. Nothing is more common in business than unsuccessful people with good ideas. The long, bumpy and often winding road from idea to financial pay-off is what creates success. There are no shortcuts.

Pay less tax—legitimately

Speak to a good accountant to understand what deductions are available to you. Check that your accountant hasn't missed anything. I know that when I review new clients' financial statements, I find, on average, $5000 of tax savings that have been ignored through lazy bookkeeping—$5000 every year, going to waste.

Consolidate debt onto your mortgage

As part of the structure I recommend to my clients, outstanding debts should be consolidated onto your mortgage. Although this means you will owe more on your mortgage, you will pay less interest overall—all your credit card debt and personal loans would now be at mortgage interest rates. Importantly, without other payments dragging on your income, you will be able to apply more of your surplus income to the mortgage.

While debt consolidation can be a good strategy, it is only effective as long as you do not accrue further debt. The long-term impact of adding extra costs to your mortgage can actually be more expensive if the overall debt is not paid off. This is one of the reasons I provide ongoing monitoring and support to my clients, to ensure that debt levels reduce as fast as projections indicated they could, and why it is so important to keep a close watch on your finances.

If you have insufficient equity at your existing bank to consolidate other debts onto the mortgage, then consider refinancing with another bank.

Debt consolidation—no mortgage

If you do not have a mortgage, it may be worthwhile consolidating your credit card balances to one low interest rate. Some banks allow you to transfer the balance of your credit card for as little as 2.99 per cent for the first six months. However, after six months the interest rate might increase. Some banks allow you to have the low-interest rate for the length of time it takes you to repay the transferred balance.

It is important, if you are transferring your balance, that you use the respite of lower outgoings to repay the debt balance faster.

If you are unable to consolidate your debts, the best approach is to rank all debts according to interest rates. Pay the debts off in order of interest rates, paying the debts at the highest rates first.

Structure your debt better

Look at interest rates and different terms—compare banks. Factoring in break costs and possible penalties, should you change the length of your fixed term? Should you refinance to another bank? I had one client who was being charged interest at a rate of 10 per cent per annum at one bank, who successfully refinanced to another bank at 7 per cent. In this case no break costs applied. Remember each bank has slightly different lending criteria. What is a negative for one bank might not be onerous to another.

But, unless you are recording and tracking everything, and unless your plan is tied to achieving actual results, you may feel as if you have made a concession without having anything to show for it.

> Recording and tracking your progress will keep you motivated—provided you achieve results.

Avoid revolving credit mortgages

Revolving credit—or revolting credit as I call it—mortgages are a license for disguised overspending and an increase in your mortgage balance over time. Your mortgage is set up as a large overdraft (using standard mortgage rates) that is supposed to reduce over time faster than a standard 30-year mortgage due to the following assumptions. Your income is directed into the overdraft, reducing the balance of the overdraft and the interest that is charged. You then spend from the overdraft. The money that you leave in the overdraft (i.e. do not spend) reduces the overdraft and saves you interest. Further savings are supposed to be had if you pay for your living costs on a credit card, which results in your income sitting against the overdraft for longer. This lowers the overdraft balance, and reduces your interest costs as the interest is charged on the balance of the overdraft. Technically they sound like a dream but in reality, they can be a nightmare. Living off your credit card is a recipe for disaster irrespective of whether you can afford to repay your credit in full at the end of the month. Repayment of your credit card is not the trick to success. The trick is your mortgage balance reducing over time, and reducing as fast as it possibly can. Most people do not reduce their mortgage, and of those that do 95 per cent are not reducing it as fast as they could.

The fact is that most of us shouldn't use this type of mortgage as we do not have the discipline to use it to our advantage. Further, this type of mortgage uses a floating rate and this tends to be higher than a fixed rate. It means people are exposing themselves to a higher interest rate for the ability to repay debt faster, but in most instances are not paying off their debt any faster because they don't have any money left over after they've paid off their credit cards. They're unable to tap into the advantages this type of credit should offer, so the only one who wins is the bank.

Repay your debts

Any spare cash should be channelled into repaying debts faster. So much money is wasted on paying interest and servicing loans. Chose one loan to focus on at a time and pay it off fast. As you repay each loan, channel the newly available funds that no longer need to be allocated to the repaid loan into paying off the next debt. Remember to pay debts off in order of interest rate. Higher interest rates should be prioritised as a rule of thumb.

Groceries

Plan your meals, write a list and stick to it. If you struggle to stick to a tight shopping budget, consider shopping online as it allows you to sort by specials. Online shopping for groceries also eliminates the spur-of-the-moment items—usually expensive treats—that get thrown into your trolley as you walk the aisles of the supermarket.

Electricity supply

Compare prices from electricity providers, but be sure to build in dividends you might receive by staying with a certain provider.

CASH IS KING

Whether you are a business or an individual, you have to have enough money coming in to cover your bills and still have money left over. If you cannot afford to pay your bills with real money, you have a problem.

I do not recommend that you pay in kind, or pay using contra deals (exchanging goods or products instead of money). You cannot pay your mortgage or tax with a cash substitute and that makes them high risk. If you want to avoid using credit, you have to start using cash.

The key to getting ahead starts with having cash left over as the surplus cash becomes the springboard for financial progress. Your wealth builds from this cash surplus.

If you are going to develop a budget, first find where the money is going so you can catch it before it is spent. Do not rely on your instincts for this—you will be spending more than you realise across a number of different costs. Print out bank statements and actually look at where the money has gone. This is an analysis of spending—it is not a budget. From this analysis you can start to build a budget. (See Appendix III for a budget template you can use.)

If your list of expenses shows that you do not have enough money coming in to cover all your costs, it will show as a deficit. A deficit means that you are going backwards. It is all too common to fund this financial backsliding with credit cards and mortgage top-ups. This is where some people go wrong—they assume that because someone is prepared to give them credit they should use it.

Many people think that the bank wouldn't give you money if they didn't think you should use it. Unfortunately, the link between what you can afford and what a bank is prepared to lend you is surprisingly weak. I have heard clients say countless times, 'If only the bank hadn't given me the money, I wouldn't be in this situation.'

Remember, no-one cares about your financial situation as much as you. Don't rely on other people to make financial decisions for you, and try not to blame them even if they have facilitated your financial demise. Your personal banker has no idea about your overall financial situation, your money personality, your relationship or your longer-term goals. Nor are they qualified to give independent advice, so please don't rely on what they say. In fact, there is a clear conflict of interest for anyone giving you advice where they gain a benefit from the amount of debt you incur.

Clients buying a property ask me, 'What can I borrow?' They are actually asking two questions in one—How much will the bank lend me, and how much can I afford to service (or pay back)? The two questions usually give materially different answers. Usually, banks are prepared to lend you more money than you can comfortably afford to pay back. This means you will have to drastically alter your lifestyle to absorb the higher debt repayments, or you'll start to go backwards.

Although most New Zealanders are spending more than they earn—pre-GFC we spent, on average, $1.15 for every dollar we earned—this is not the time to be following the herd. You cannot achieve the perfect balance financially until you have a cash surplus—a real cash-sitting-in-the-bank, cash surplus.

I had a client who filled in a budget that showed she had an annual $50 000 cash surplus. She came to see me and said that she was not getting ahead. I asked where the surplus was, knowing that if it were a legitimate surplus, the $50 000 would be sitting in a bank account somewhere. It was nowhere to be seen. Her reply was, 'I can't find it, but I know that you will be able to find it, and it will then be okay.'

In reality, her cash surplus had been frittered on things. It was being spent on little things often. She spent because she could, she had no reason not to. As with any financial situation, unless there is a cash surplus you cannot start to make lasting improvements to your lifestyle or wealth. That was her first step—to find where her supposed surplus was going. Next, my suggestion was that she develop a budget and slash it until she had a real cash surplus. Then she had to try and stick to the budget.

This client did not have the time or the inclination to find this information out for herself, so she outsourced this to me. This is an option for those who are time-poor. Someone has to take responsibility for your cash position. I recognise that some of you may not have the time or interest in doing it for yourself, so you need to delegate this to someone who will.

If you follow this simple guideline correctly, you should start to systematically build a cash surplus. For example, if your cash surplus was $12,000 per annum you should start to save at around $1000 per month. If you cannot see the result at the end of each month, you are not doing it correctly. Cash is an asset—as you build your cash, you are starting to build wealth.

> Remember, the purpose of a budget isn't to determine where your money went, but where your money should go.

PROGRESS IS QUEEN

It is not enough to take steps that may, some day, lead to a goal. Each step you take must in itself be a goal, too.

If cash is king, then progress is queen. After you have established that you can reliably spend less than you earn, you need to take that surplus and invest it. Do something with it to increase its value. To increase your wealth, you have the option of acquiring assets, such as saving or investing in businesses and shares. Alternatively, you could repay debt or mortgages faster.

If you had $100 and saved it, or took the same amount and reduced your debt by $100, it would have the same effect on your wealth.

It is not simply about the value of your assets, or the

size of your debt. It is the relationship between the two that is important—it is your net position that determines your wealth. A lot of people may consider themselves asset-rich, but if their debt is at a similar level to their assets, overall they might not be worth much.

As an exercise, list all your assets and list all your debts. Subtract your debts from your assets to establish your overall wealth. To be an asset something needs to hold its value or increase in value. Cars, which depreciate quickly, do not usually count for much when calculating your wealth.

You need cash savings to build sufficiently before retirement, so you can live off it during retirement. Many of my clients leave their run to sort their finances until the eleventh hour. They might come to see me for the first time just before they turn sixty. They may have eight or nine years to retirement, and still 20 years until they are mortgage-free. In this instance we might need to take an aggressive stance to prepare them for retirement, as putting aside 10 per cent of what they earn between then and retirement is not going to cut it. Each situation is slightly different. If you are starting out early enough, saving 10 per cent wisely and leaving it untouched should do the trick.

I have had a few clients who have come to see me at age 65 who still have a 'couple of years of work in them'. Even at this age, I can still work with people to help them achieve their financial goals. Time isn't on our side, so I have to adjust my usual advice, but their goals can be achieved nonetheless.

I recall the initial meeting with a 60-year-old client who cried when I asked her how long until her mortgage was repaid. Her answer—'Twenty years.' She also told me she had no savings for retirement. Next I asked her if she was prepared to sort this once and for all. Her answer was a determined 'yes'.

Even if you are starting on the back foot and time is against you, you can still achieve your goals if you are prepared to do whatever is necessary. If you do not have much time to sort your retirement plan, you need to take smart, fast steps in the right direction to achieve your goal. Everything needs to be working together to ensure you leapfrog forward. While not many people actually start on the journey to improve their finances, fewer people in fact reach their destination within the time allocated. Setting off in the right direction does not ensure that you will arrive at the sought-after destination. Purposeful steps, day after day, in line with your tailored road, is what will get you there.

WEALTH

There is a Texan saying, 'Big hat, no cattle'. It describes people who looked like cowboys, had all the right gear, but owned no cattle themselves. They looked the part, but behind the facade, there was nothing of financial substance. The Kiwi version is probably, 'Looking good, but going nowhere.' This resonates with many people and probably best describes a number of people's financial situations. You don't feel like you are going backwards, but you also do not have a sense of reaching your financial potential.

Most people, when they think of wealth or being wealthy, would describe the term as 'having an abundance of material possessions'. This is consistent with most definitions. But, like most things in finance, things are not always what they seem. Being wealthy does not necessarily mean owning a lot of material possessions. In fact, many people who display such a lifestyle tend to have little or no investments, appreciable assets, businesses, or income-producing assets. Most people who are high consumers living in a big house have a big mortgage, too.

An easy way to determine if someone is wealthy is to base it on net worth—cattle, not chattels.

If progress is queen, are you joining the royal family? Are you getting ahead? It is a yes–no question. Remove the emotion—how you feel is irrelevant. Have you made progress or not? If not, things need to change.

> **Example:** Trish has a home worth $600000 and savings of $10000. She has a mortgage of $550000 and credit card debt of $10000. Right now, Trish is worth $50000. This is her net wealth.
>
> Trish has a cash surplus of $10000 per annum. This means that her wealth should be increasing by $10000 per annum. She can either deposit this as cash surplus as an extra saving, or she can reduce her debt by

$10 000 every year. Both will increase her wealth, or net position, by $10 000 to $60 000 at the end of the year. In Trish's scenario the $50 000 of existing wealth is the result of paying off some of the principal on her mortgage, $10 000, and capital gain on their property, $40 000 since she purchased it. She purchased the property with a 100 per cent loan as she had no deposit saved.

More often than not, it is easier to reduce debt than increase assets. Psychologically it seems easier as people are more motivated to avoid interest than to earn interest. Another reason to reduce debt is that the interest rate on debt tends to be higher than the interest rate you can earn from a savings account or term deposit. Your 10 per cent saved can go towards savings or repaying debt, but repaying debt usually saves you more than your savings can earn and therefore makes your money go further.

When considering what debt to repay, as a general rule you need to look to repay the debt with the highest interest rate, as this debt is costing you the most. Exceptions to this may be when you have a number of debts outstanding and you cannot successfully consolidate the debts into one loan, or it is not worth your while doing this as the interest rate and monthly repayments on the consolidated loan are higher than your current payments.

Family loans, although they may have no interest being charged, can still feel like a 'monkey on your back' and create anxiety or a sense of pressure. In these instances, it may be appropriate to clear that debt first, on the proviso that you will be able to get ahead faster without the additional emotional pressure that debt may have brought. Removing the anxiety and pressure would certainly improve your overall wellbeing and lifestyle.

WHAT TO DO WITH YOUR MONEY

If you have managed to save 10 per cent of your income, say $20 000, you need to invest this money to increase its worth, and to increase your wealth. You have a number of options of what to do with the money, but for most people putting it in the bank is the best thing to do until you have adequately researched your other options. The objective is that you use the money saved to make more money. In the bank the money will earn interest. This interest will be added to the money earned and the increased amount will be reinvested. The balance will grow and, provided you continue to live within your means, and it is left untouched, it will start to grow exponentially. This is when compound interest starts to kick in.

However, remember that if you have a mortgage it often pays to apply your savings to repaying debt, as the interest charges you will be avoiding can often exceed the interest you would earn from putting your savings in the bank.

COMPOUND INTEREST

Compound interest really is magical. It's said that Albert Einstein once declared it to be the most powerful force in the universe. It consists of putting money into an account and letting it earn interest from that moment on. This process of getting interest on the interest earned is called compound interest. Over the short term compound interest is not all that exciting. But over longer time periods, the results are impressive and obvious.

If you put $1000 in the bank and draw 5 per cent interest, then at the end of the year you will have $1050. If you leave the entire amount in the bank for another year you will then have $1103. In the second year, not only did you get interest on the original investment, but you also got interest on the interest you earned the prior year. This is when compound interest kicks in. Compound interest is of relevance to anyone leaving their investment to grow over a long period of time. The $1000 investment mentioned above, when invested for 40 years at 5 per cent, will be worth over $7000!

The following 40-year investment chart shows how the future value of an investment grows most spectacularly in the later years. In this example, half of the future value is earned in the last ten years. Mortgages are the same, but in reverse. If you commit to the bank's predetermined mortgage length (25 or 30 years), you are not going to start making obvious dents into the loan balance until the last ten years. Over time the sensitivity of interest rates becomes more pronounced, the longer the term.

At first glance it might be tempting to say that the difference between investing at 5 per cent and 6 per cent would not be significant. However, an increase of a single percentage point on an investment can result in a 50 per cent increase in the future value of an investment over a 40-year period.

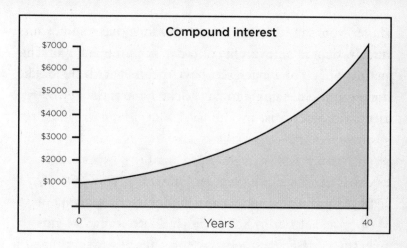

The frequency at which interest is applied to an investment account can be important. The more frequently the interest is charged, the better for savings growth. Most compound interest projections assume that interest is added annually. But there are opportunities to earn interest daily, monthly or quarterly.

The following table compares the effect of compounding interest monthly, quarterly, and yearly. The table is for a $1000 investment over 40 years.

Interest Rate	Yearly	Quarterly	Monthly
5%	$7040	$7298	$7358
10%	$45 259	$51 978	$53 700

At 5 per cent, interest compounded monthly results in a 5 per cent increase in future value as compared to interest compounded yearly.

Compound interest works nicely with savings—the

longer you save for, the more exciting the result. Conversely, debt is an example of compound interest working against you. The longer you have the debt with the bank, the more you are going to pay back. Time is the key ingredient. Consider this:

Jim is 20 years old. He saves $1000 per annum every year for the next ten years. He then stops saving, but does not withdraw any savings. He leaves his savings in the bank account until he turns 65. His savings are earning interest at 5 per cent per annum. The interest earned is added to the savings made each year. When he turns 65, he has $81834 sitting in his savings account.

Kathy is 35. She also starts saving $1000 per annum. She continues this saving regime until she is 65, so over that 30-year period she has physically saved $30000. Like Jim, the interest she is earning over time is added to the savings balance. She also is earning interest at 5 per cent per annum. When she turns 65 she has saved $74082.

So Kathy saves $20000 more than Jim, but earns $7752 less.

The moral of this story is not to marry someone fifteen years younger than you but instead to get started on things sooner rather than later. Compound interest respects no man or woman, but is dictated to by time.

Saving $20 per week from the age of twenty

Start saving $20 a week when you're twenty and by the time you're 60 you'll have $41 600 saved. Each year you are saving $1040, which is $5200 every five years. This doesn't change. But can you see that the interest you are earning grows exponentially, so that by the time you are 60, you have physically saved $41 600 but you have $70 280 in the bank. This is assuming an interest rate of 5%.

Age	Savings	Interest*	Balance in bank account at the end of the year*
25	$5200	$709	$5909
30	$10 400	$1341	$1741
35	$15 600	$4352	$19 952
40	$20 800	$7290	$35 290
45	$26 000	$10 829	$36 829
50	$31 200	$15 371	$46 571
55	$36 400	$21 200	$57 600
60	$41 600	$28 680	$70 280

* Rounded to the nearest dollar

Saving $60 a week from the age of twenty

If you started saving $60 a week from the age of twenty, using the same interest rate as above you would have $210 841 in the bank by the time you were sixty. Here we can really see how the power of compound interest makes your money grow! You will have physically saved $124 800 after 40 years, but will have an astonishing $210 841 in the bank.

Age	Savings	Interest*	Balance in bank account at the end of the year*
25	$15 600	$2127	$17 727
30	$31 200	$7150	$38 350
35	$46 800	$13 596	$60 396
40	$62 400	$21 869	$84 269
45	$78 000	$32 487	$110 487
50	$93 600	$46 112	$139 712
55	$109 200	$63 599	$172 799
60	$124 800	$86 041	$210 841

* Rounded to the nearest dollar

MORTGAGES

While I am sure that there are a number of us who like to see our wealth increase, the main purpose of wealth is to allow you to live a lifestyle you enjoy—to live in a home you like, to drive the car you want, take holidays when you feel, and to enjoy yourself during retirement. One of the key ways of preparing for retirement is to have purchased a home and repaid the mortgage well before you stop working. The reason for this is twofold. If you don't own your own home you have to pay rent, so you have an outgoing no matter what. Whether you pay rent to someone else, or continue to pay off a mortgage, the money is still leaving your bank account. The beauty about being mortgage-free is that the money that was paying off the mortgage no longer leaves your bank account, allowing you to save more while you are still working. You will also spend less in your retirement, so your savings will last longer.

Getting a mortgage can be easy. Getting rid of it can be more of a challenge. Getting rid of your mortgage is discussed in more detail later (see page 128 of Chapter 4).

CAPITAL GAIN

Although property values go up and down depending on the status of the economy and the timing in the property cycle, over time they consistently appreciate. If you are a tenant, your rent increases by around 2 per cent every year. This is usually because the landlord is passing on the cost of inflation. If you are a home owner your mortgage payments do not increase with inflation. This is a gain to you. In fact, you benefit from inflation as the property increases in value but your debt remains static. This means the real value of the debt reduces over time.

Consider this example: You bought a property in 1975 for $20 000 and at that time you were earning $10 000 per annum. That same property is now worth $600 000. If you borrowed 100 per cent of the value of the property at the time of purchase and only paid interest your debt is still $20000. The $20000 is a fraction of your total income now, 30 years later.

TEACHING CHILDREN ABOUT FINANCIAL LITERACY

It has been proved that the more dollars adult children are given by family, the fewer they accumulate by themselves as adults—on the other side of that coin, those who are given less accumulate more.[14] Even though it has been proven to be untrue, many parents still think that their wealth can automatically make their children economically productive adults.

If you continue to fund your children, even if you have the best of intentions, you are in fact disadvantaging them by subsidising their lifestyle—letting them spend more than they need or that they can truly afford.

It is also interesting to consider some of the most successful business owners around. They are the people who have put their money where their mouths are. They have backed themselves and invested their own resources in their own ideas. They have succeeded because they had to succeed. It was their money, their time, their product and their reputation—and there were no safety nets. They had no-one else to rely on for their success.

No matter how wealthy you are, teach your children discipline and frugality. Remember though, kids are smart. They will not follow rules that their parents themselves do not follow.

It is not easy to make money so treat it with respect. Teach your children the value of money. The sooner anyone understands the value of money, the more likely they are to possess large sums of it in their adult lives.

If your children see you being careless with money, they too will become careless. Not teaching your children about money is not caring. Most things in this life are either directly or indirectly linked to money, so understanding and valuing money is a necessary life skill. You need money to survive.

I have many clients who cry when they first meet with me and say, 'I have turned out just like my parents', or 'I am so scared I am going to turn out just like my parents'.

This may be an accurate diagnosis of their financial situation, but that does not mean they can't change their situation. You can help them by first taking the time to correct your behaviour and teaching them what you have learned so your children, for the most part, won't repeat the same financial mistakes you have made.

Poor money skills can screw up your kids. Good money skills and habits, on the other hand, can insulate your kids from making major mistakes later in life. These lessons will positively impact on their quality of life as adults. According to Neale S. Godfrey, author of *Money Doesn't Grow on Trees: A parent's guide to raising financially responsible children*, a disappointingly high 20 per cent of parents never speak to their kids about the basics of money.[15]

To raise money-smart kids, parents should start at a young age and regularly reinforce money lessons as children grow up. Unlike a birds-and-bees or don't-do-drugs speech, money skills must be taught to kids, experienced hands-on and consistently modelled by parents. However, the reality for most parents is that they don't have the skills themselves to teach their children.

To avoid setting your kids up for financial failure, before they leave home teach them these four things:

- How to budget

- How to make and follow through on spending decisions

- How to appreciate the rewards of their work

- How to delay gratification.

Teaching children how to budget

Because the foundation of success comes down to budgeting, this is the first lesson to be learned. Budgeting has to start with money, and that means putting cash in kids' hands.

Making and following through on spending decisions

Though giving and saving are important skills to master, good money habits start with spending. That's where all the action is and where all the most valuable lessons are to be learned.

Let your children make mistakes and don't bail them out when they have gone wrong. They might want to impulse buy, even if you know they will need the money for something more important to them later. As parents we want to avoid our children making mistakes, but when it comes to money, this is the best way to learn. And best they learn now, when the stakes are small and board is free. But if they make mistakes, show them where they have gone wrong and better yet, how they can get back in the zone.

Understanding the rewards of work

While paying pocket money, also teach kids that money has to be earned—additional chores can be offered for extra money so that kids learn to work for their pay. This gives them a little more control over how fast they'll be able to save up for special purchases.

Delaying gratification

You will be able to see your child's money personality from a very young age. That said, saving for a goal helps children develop their ability to delay gratification. Dividing savings into long- and short-term goals can also help kids realise that saving isn't just about spending at some point in the near future.

Putting away money just for the sake of a rainy day is a routine that every person would do well to follow, and the earlier that concept sinks in, the better. It's a lesson that continually eludes many adults.

Building budgeting skills as children get older

As kids get older, the lessons can grow more complicated. If you think your kids are ready to take on more responsibility, help them understand more about the family's finances. I encourage clients to bring their children to financial planning meetings with me so they can get a better sense of how their family manages its money.

It is good for them to learn that there are limited funds, and that specific costs have to be covered. It is also good to have a family reward if you are hitting your quarterly or annual targets. This gives the kids something to buy into and helps them accept the spending concessions their parents may be forced to make.

A popular idea with my clients is to take their teenager grocery shopping with them, telling them the budget and working through a shopping list together. If they come in under budget, I encourage them to split the saving in half, giving their teenager half and keeping the other half. In this situation, teenagers suddenly start paying attention to what things cost.

If you are doing well financially, talk to your kids about it. Explain to them how you made your money and what you intend to do with that money. Most importantly reiterate that it is your money, not theirs, but you intend to manage it wisely, so that they are looked after in the future.

I suggest to parents they cover the necessities, such as standard clothing, food, education and transport costs. Estimate how much money is spent on non-essential costs, such as mobile phones, movies, iTunes, label clothes and eating out. Assign chores so your children can earn money for the discretionary items, or extras, that you aren't prepared to buy.

Never get in the habit of giving money without them earning it as it sets the wrong tone to money management. In the majority of instances kids will spend your money more freely than their own, so don't volunteer your eftpos card. Set budgets together and stick to them. Refine the budget if you need to incorporate other costs, but stick to the plan. There is limited money coming in, so both you and your children need to understand that only limited funds can go out.

If kids can master these lessons on a small scale with their allowance, then they'll likely have the discipline and money skills to resist the lure of credit and living beyond their means in their adult lives.

Chapter 4

Buying your first home

If you're like most first-time home buyers, you've probably listened to friends and family and looked to the media for advice, much of it encouraging you to buy a home. In New Zealand in particular, people love buying property. It accounts for half the net wealth of New Zealand households. I believe we have more money locked up in property than all other asset classes put together, including superannuation, life insurance and shares. House prices seem to keep increasing, yet salaries are not increasing at the same rate. This means it is going to get harder and harder to buy your first home. But as soon as you buy a property you join the property wave and start to benefit from the increasing prices. For some the idea of buying their first property is intimidating and the process of home ownership unfamiliar. The more you know about why you should own a home, and what to expect in home ownership, the less frightening the entire process will seem. There are many benefits to owning property, some financial, some emotional. Although it is important to go into property ownership with your eyes open, there are clear reasons why getting on the property ladder is important.

Property tends to increase in value quicker than savings in the bank. Further, properties are not easily converted into cash, so as they increase in value, it is harder to spend the increase in value than accessing a savings account might be. Most properties have ways that you can increase their value independent of the property cycle, through small DIY initiatives. Instead of paying rent, you are paying down a mortgage. It is still an outgoing, but at the end of 20 or 30 years you are going to own something for yourself instead of creating profit for your landlord. Psychologically, pride of ownership is a driving force for people wanting to own their home. The property is yours to do as you see fit, to express yourself with and live a lifestyle you decide within, instead of being curtained by your landlord. You can change the look and feel of the property according to your taste, without having to ask permission. Home ownership gives you and your family a sense of stability and security. It's making an investment in your future.

WHY YOU NEED TO GET STARTED

House prices are growing faster than salaries. The following graph shows the increase in New Zealand house prices to annual gross income from 1997 to 2011.[16]

New Zealand house prices have massively increased in comparison to incomes from about 2001. Back in the early 1990s the ratio was only around 4:1, which then increased to 5:1 by the year 1998 and then it simply took off—peaking at just under 8:1 at the height of the housing mania in late 2007. It is currently around 7:1. This means that the average property is costing seven times the average wage, making it more and more unaffordable. What this says is that over the past 20 years, house price growth has outstripped wage growth five times. This is one of the reasons why it is seen as important to own property—it only gets harder to climb onto the property ladder. Many analysts think it is unsustainable for property values to stay as high as they are, but until the cost of building a home and net migration reduce, I cannot see how it will correct itself. That said, never pay more than a property is worth, and if possible negotiate a discount up front so you can make an immediate equity gain.

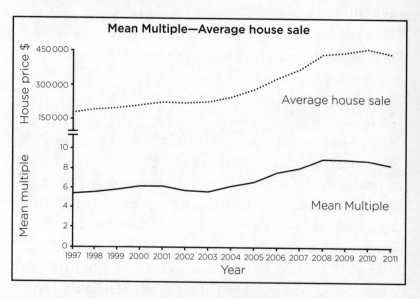

In most instances, as a first-home buyer you need to have saved around 10 per cent of the property value. The bank will lend you the rest. Provided you have a good savings history and a high enough income to pass their servicing test, the rest is pretty easy.

The bank lends you the money and you pay it back over a period of time, usually 25–30 years. You pay interest at a nominated rate for the money provided. Each month, part of your monthly payment is applied to the principal balance of your loan, which reduces your debt. With an amortised mortgage the 'principal' portion of your total mortgage payment (principal plus interest) increases slightly every month. It is lowest on your first payment and highest on your last payment. On average, each $100 000 of principal will reduce in the first year of a standard table mortgage by about $500, bringing the balance owing to $99 500 at the end of the first 12 months.

It is important to reduce your mortgage as fast as possible to reduce the overall interest costs.

LEVELS OF RISK

There is no such thing as no risk when it comes to putting your money to some use or investing it. It is said that investing in the bank at a conservative term deposit rate is the safest form of wealth creation or investment. This is because it is assumed the lending institution—usually a bank—has sufficient income to pay back your deposit if asked. Generally that is the case, but not all banks are created equal, as evidenced by the recent global financial crisis (GFC). Putting the GFC to one side, the inherent disadvantage of investing in a bank is that the returns are low. This makes sense because there is less risk. For many, the returns in the bank are not enough to meet their financial goals so they set about looking at other investments.

The key to investing is you understanding what you are investing in. Because we have some of the lowest financial literacy in the developed world, we are attracted to what we understand and know will work.

Property ticks this box. Looking back over time we can see that the typical family home with a reasonable section has consistently increased in value in most cases. We also like the fact that a house and section is a physical asset. It is appealing that even if the market crashes you will still own the asset—provided you keep paying the mortgage.

The same cannot be said for investment in businesses and financial institutions as many people learned the hard way after the GFC—many businesses and banks are no longer around for people to collect their money. What's more, you can insure a house. So even when natural disasters strike, such as the Christchurch earthquakes, you have ring-fenced and protected your wealth against natural disaster.

Not all properties increase in value at the same rate. Some properties that do not own any land—for example, apartments or leasehold buildings—may not increase in value at all. But in general, for your typical family home in a good area near good schools you can expect an increase in value over time. This increase is greater than any gain you could have earned if you had invested the money in a bank, yet it is not perceived as being significantly more risky.

GETTING YOUR FIRST MORTGAGE

If you're considering purchasing a home in the near future you need to be up to speed on getting a mortgage, from the pre-approval to how to use the mortgage to your benefit once you have bought your first home. For many, getting a mortgage is easier than you think. Banks tend to chomp at the bit to give you a mortgage to buy a house. They are usually guilty of giving you more money than you can comfortably afford to repay. It is noted, however, that since the GFC bank lending has tightened, which means that they are less likely to lend you money unless you have a saved deposit. This seems logical, but it is in contrast to the lead-up to the GFC when banks were handing out money to people who never should have qualified for a mortgage, which no doubt contributed to the problem.

To get a mortgage you need to have the following:

- A saved deposit of at least 10 per cent. Some banks will lower this to 5 per cent if you look like a good customer

- Good account conduct—not going into unarranged overdrafts, etc.

- Solid and consistent employment. It is usually harder for the self-employed to get a mortgage, unless they have been in business for a few years and their financial statements show a strong and reliable profit

- The ability to pay the mortgage against bank calculators, which often use a higher interest rate than the current interest rates on offer, to try and build in contingency for interest rate fluctuations over time

- It can help if you already bank with the bank you are seeking a mortgage from, but this is no longer a priority as a bank's loyalty to their customers seems to count for little nowadays

- Good credit ratings—no unpaid fines, etc.

Your credit rating is crucial. Check in with Baycorp <http://baycorp.co.nz> to see if there is anything unusual appearing on your credit history. If you have any unpaid fines, pay them.

HOW MUCH CAN YOU AFFORD?

Banks are usually happy to lend you money if they are comfortable that you can afford the repayments. But, in determining your ability to repay they use their bank's calculators. This calculator applies in-house rules to determine whether, according to the bank, you can afford the loan. These calculators allocate pre-determined living costs to you, and disregard what your actual living costs might be. They build margins into the interest rates to exaggerate interest repayments. They tend to discount some income streams like rent, or disregard other legitimate income types; for example, child support. This can mean that by your calculations you can afford a property, while the bank might say no, or conversely that the bank's calculations indicate you can service a higher mortgage than your lifestyle really allows. That said, in theory it is in the bank's interest for you to be able to pay your mortgage, so you would expect that they would lend you only what they believe you can afford to repay (or for what they can insure their loans for).

Have a chat to your bank if you are unsure, or use the spreadsheets at the back of this book (see page 211) to run your own mortgage calculations.

In most instances banks will require you to have saved a 10 per cent deposit. For example, if a property is worth $500 000 you would need to have a $50 000 deposit. Whether you have been given this money by your parents or saved it yourself doesn't seem to make too much difference. There are some instances where banks are still happy to lend 100 per cent of the purchase price, but these are now very much the exception to the rule.

Debt-to-income ratios give lenders a quick rule of thumb to determine how much they can borrow. They try to keep loans affordable by keeping payments to a modest percentage of your total income. However, because house prices have increased beyond the increase in income, the debt-to-income ratio that is now accepted is considerably higher than 20 years ago. Using debt-to-income ratios, lenders can quickly figure out a reasonable monthly payment and use that number to calculate the total amount they will lend—the loan amount.

HOUSING EXPENSE DEBT-TO-INCOME RATIO

Your housing expense debt-to-income ratio measures the percentage of your income that covers mortgage payments. Lenders set certain limits for your debt-to-income ratio. For example, they might say they want your housing expenses to be less than 50 per cent of your gross monthly income. So, if you earn $6000 per month gross—before taxes—and your bank wants your debt-to-income ratio to be below 40 per cent, the calculation of the upper limit of your monthly mortgage payments will be:

$$6000 \times 0.4 = 2400$$

In other words, your lender wants you to spend $2400 or less per month on mortgage payments.

To work out how much debt this allows, you need to annualise the monthly mortgage payment and then divide by the average interest rate:

$$2400 \times 12 = 28\,800$$

$$28\,800 \div 7\% = 411\,400*$$

(* rounded to the nearest $100)

Therefore, $411 400 is the maximum your lender will let you borrow.

If you're a first-time home buyer, and you have been in KiwiSaver for three years or more, you may be able to access some of your KiwiSaver balance. Check in with your local KiwiSaver provider.

I believe you should maximise the length of your mortgage term, then find a way to voluntarily repay it faster, as funds are available. (See 'Getting rid of your mortgage' on page 128.) A 30-year fixed-rate mortgage is generally the safest and best bet, especially if you expect to live in your house for more than five years or so.

SHOULD I FIX OR FLOAT?

When you take out a mortgage, you usually have the option of fixing or floating the interest rate. Typically, a fixed rate is lower than a floating rate, although that is not always the case. With a fixed interest loan the interest rate you pay is fixed for a period from six months to five years (some banks can allow you to fix for up to ten years, but this is not common). At the end of the term, a fixed interest loan should automatically move to the floating rate, with your monthly repayments changing to reflect the new rate. Be careful on this point though. Where the floating rate is lower than the fixed rate, not all banks automatically reduce your repayments to reflect the lower payment, instead requiring you to sign off on the repayment amount. Unsurprisingly, though, if the floating rate is higher than the previously fixed rate they will automatically increase your repayments to reflect this. It is possible at some banks to negotiate a new fixed interest loan up to six weeks prior to the expiry of the existing fixed term without incurring any break costs or penalties.

The key benefits to fixing your loan are that you know exactly what your monthly or fortnightly repayment will be, making it easier to budget for. The repayment amount does not change during the period of your fixed interest term, irrespective of what is happening in the global economy or changes in our domestic interest rates. So you can lock in lower rates for longer if the market interest rates are rising. Further, rates tend to be lower than the floating rate (normally by 1–1.5 per cent). The main disadvantage is that you cannot easily repay principal back faster without incurring penalties, or the amount you can repay is pre-set by the bank. Further, if you were to pay it back, you cannot easily re-access the funds voluntarily applied to the mortgage in an emergency. That said, most New Zealanders do not have surplus funds to invest in their mortgage, so the idea of not being able to pay the loan back faster is no real disadvantage.

Floating rates, on the other hand, are variable, and can change regularly, often without warning. Banks can increase or decrease rates at their discretion, although this is usually dictated by the wider market changes. Interest rate changes affect your repayments, meaning that your repayment amount will increase if rates are increasing, and decrease if rates reduce. Where fluctuations are not foreseen, or no buffer exists in your budget to cover these movements, the ramifications can be huge. The key benefit of floating rates is that for the few in a position to repay their mortgage faster than their current mortgage repayments dictate, you are able to repay the loan at your discretion without incurring any penalties from the bank.

It is also possible to split a loan between fixed and floating rates. This lets you make extra repayments without charge on the floating rate portion while you get lower rates on the fixed portion. For most people though, although this may seem like a good idea, if you are not in a position to make extra payments on your mortgage because you have no cash surplus, then there is no point having a floating mortgage or exposing yourself to a higher interest rate for the sake of being able to repay the loan without penalty when repayment is not a viable option.

How long you fix a loan for will depend on your situation, what interest rates are doing generally and what your goals are. If you intend to stay in your house for the next few years and interest rates are increasing, it would make sense to lock in a lower interest rate for as long as you can afford. The average interest rate over ten years is 8 per cent, so if you can afford it there is an argument for fixing for as long as possible provided the rate you are fixing is below the long-term average of 8 per cent.

If, however, you intend to sell your home in 18 months, there is little sense fixing for longer than 18 months, as you may be exposed to break costs or penalties when you eventually sell the house and repay the mortgage.

HOW FREQUENTLY SHOULD I PAY MY MORTGAGE?

You have the option of paying your mortgage weekly, fortnightly or monthly. In general, people match their payment frequency with their income frequency. So if you are paid weekly, pay your mortgage off weekly. If you are paid fortnightly, set up your mortgage payments to be made fortnightly, etc.

Some people believe there is a secret saving by making payments weekly or fortnightly versus monthly. Yes, you can pay your mortgage off faster if you are making payments fortnightly versus monthly. The reason for this is because you make an extra payment under the fortnightly repayments than you would have made when paying monthly over a twelve-month period. There are twelve months in each year, but 26 fortnights. If there were 24 fortnightly payments per annum, there would be no mortgage repayment difference between the two frequencies. The extra fortnightly payments do reduce your debt a bit faster, although saving for that extra fortnightly payment can be stressful (especially if you are paid monthly).

When working with clients, I place little importance on the frequency selected, instead focusing on channelling all surplus money to the mortgage.

SHOULD I BREAK MY MORTGAGE?

Interest rates are nice and low at the moment, but the only people who benefit from this are people who are on a floating interest rate. If you are unlucky enough to still be on a high interest rate when current rates are low it can be tempting to break your existing contract and take a new contract at today's rate at another bank. While you can do this, often there is a cost or a penalty for breaking a contract early.

Break costs act as a deterrent for breaking your loan early. They are designed to neutralise any gain that might have been made by changing from one interest rate to another when rates fall. The penalty is prepaid to offset any future reductions in interest charged for the remaining term of the initial contract, and is calculated using a fixed formula described in very small print in your mortgage documents. The calculated fee is based on the size of the mortgage being broken and how far the comparative interest rates have fallen since the loan was first fixed, combined with how many months until the fixed interest period ends.

Although it sounds complicated, the fee roughly equates to $1000 per $100000 borrowed for every 1 per cent fall in rates, and for every year of its remaining fixed-rate term. So if interest rates fall by 3 per cent, a customer with a $300000 mortgage on a five-year fixed rate with two years still to go will face a penalty fee of around $18000—ouch!

However, there is one notable exception to this rule. If you are going to break your contract and pay the penalty, you can still make a financial gain if you are able to contract at a lower rate than that used in the penalty calculation. This can be achieved if you fix interest rates for a different term. So instead of fixing for five years (to which the break cost was first calculated), you fix for a shorter period, like three years, on the assumption the three-year interest rate was lower than the five-year interest rate. In calculating the penalty, the banks compare your fixed-rate term with today's rate for the original fixed-rate period.

For example, if you have a $400000 mortgage and have fixed your interest for five years at 8 per cent, and you are three years into the contract when you want to break it, the calculations, assuming today's five-year rate is 6 per cent, might look like this:

The difference in the five-year interest rate is 2%.

There are two years left to run on the $400000 loan.

$400000 × 0.02 × two years = $16000

Interest charged per year on $400 000 loan:

8% = $32 000

6% = $24 000

Annual difference = $8000

So if you were to break your mortgage, based on the calculations above you would pay $16 000 in break costs. Each year, for the next two years, you pay $8000 less in interest costs than you would have, so that over time you are no worse off. However, nowhere in your bank documents does it say that you have to re-fix your mortgage for the same term. So if rates were favourable on a one-, two- or three-year term, you might consider changing the interest term, to save more over the next two years.

For example, say the rate for a three-year term was 5 per cent and you decided you would fix at this rate once you had broken your contract. The penalty for breaking your contract remains $16 000. But if you fixed at 5 per cent, your interest charge would be $20 000 per annum (compared to the $32 000 it was originally). The annual interest saving equates to $12 000 for the next two years. Overall, you can see that you would gain from breaking. Yes, it will cost you $16 000 initially. But you are going to save $24 000 in interest costs over the next two years, making you $6000 in the black overall.

Remember, although the bank uses the equivalent fixed-term rate to calculate the break cost, you are not obliged to re-fix for the same term at the lower rate. Financial gain can be made if you re-fix at a lower rate than what was used to calculate the penalty, or you go to a floating rate that is less than the current five-year rate, which we assumed was 6 per cent.

Generally, banks do not charge break costs if you are breaking a contract to go onto a higher rate by comparison. This may be a way to also make savings. For example, if you were fixed for five years at 7 per cent and today's five-year rate is 8 per cent, and the two-year rate is 5 per cent, you could break your contract and not be charged a penalty, and then fix for two years at 5 per cent, making a saving.

NO-ONE IS IMMUNE TO HIGH INTEREST RATES

At some point during your mortgage, interest rates are going to be high and you are going to struggle to keep up with the payments. Those unlucky enough to have had a mortgage in the late 1980s will remember the crippling interest rates in excess of 20 per cent. If you are unlucky enough to have your mortgage fall due or your interest rate loan expire when the market is offering high rates, you might not have the option of floating your mortgage and waiting out the high rates for lower average rates to emerge. While I am not suggesting rates will go as high as 20 per cent, in the years preceding the GFC fixed rates were in excess of 10 per cent, and floating rates hit 12 per cent. Many could not afford the option of floating their mortgage and exposing themselves to higher rates, especially when the word on the street was that the floating rates were not likely to come down any time soon. So they had no option but fix, to gain what little respite they could from the slightly lower and fixed interest rate. The impact of this decision is still affecting some people. I have some clients that were fixed for five years at a rate in excess of 8.75 per cent, because this was the only rate they could afford. They didn't have the option of breaking their loans to enjoy the floating rates and lower repayments, as they did not have enough equity to pay for the break cost. So while the rest of us enjoyed historic low interest rates, they have had to ride out the storm of unfortunate timing.

You need to build your budget around the scenario of higher interest rates so you have room to move when the storm comes.

REFINANCING A MORTGAGE

There are times when you can get a better mortgage at a different bank. Perhaps it's because mortgage rates differ between banks, the equity in your property has increased or your type of property is recognised more favourably at a different bank. Whatever the reason, there can be clear, tangible and persuasive financial gains earned when refinancing for the right reasons. It makes sense to refinance your mortgage if your bank is not assisting you; for example, if interest rates are lower at a different bank and the cost of penalties to change banks is less than the future interest saving, or if your bank is not prepared to consolidate debt, meaning you are paying a higher average interest rate. Note, too, that some banks offer special interest rate discounts to certain industries, or conversely might increase interest rates if you have low equity.

I know a lot of people do not like their bank, but most banks are the same. It is worth shopping around from time to time but don't think that you are going to get radically improved service by going to another bank—this is seldom the case.

GETTING RID OF YOUR MORTGAGE

When my husband and I purchased our first property for $350 000, we needed a mortgage of $300 000. The rate was 8 per cent, so we were going to be paying close to 2.5 times what we had borrowed over the 30 years of the mortgage—that includes $490 000 in interest *plus* the original amount borrowed.

We knew we needed to be on the property ladder and although the mortgage payments were slightly higher than our rent at the time, I could see the merit in owning property. I also understood that I couldn't own property without the bank's investment in us, but $490 000 in interest seemed a lot.

While you have your mortgage, you are going to pay a lot of money to the bank. If you want to pay less to the bank, you have to become mortgage-free faster.

Each year you start to pay more and more principal, but initially, the slow rate of principal reduction can be demoralising. This is further emphasised by the annual letter from the bank confirming how much you have paid over the previous twelve months, and how little your mortgage has reduced. For example, after the first twelve months of our mortgage we had repaid $26 000 to the bank, yet the principal had only reduced by $2300. Talk about depressing!

And, sure, you are getting capital gain on your property, but it would be a whole lot easier to get ahead if you didn't have to make such high payments to the bank. Remember, the longer you are friends with your bank the more it is going to cost you. With each repayment you pay interest and some principal, so that over the course of the mortgage you would have paid off the loan and all the interest. To begin with, the money allocated to repaying your principal is small. For example, over the first twelve months of a $300 000 loan you will pay around $26 400 back to the bank. Yet at the end of the first year the debt will be $297 200. Each year, on the assumption interest rates don't change, you will continue to pay the $26 400, although more will be allocated to reducing the principal, so that over time, the principal is being reduced more and more each year.

I always assumed that in year fifteen—the halfway point in the life of the mortgage—my monthly repayments would be evenly split between interest and principal. But this was not to be the case. For any 30-year mortgage you do not start paying more principal than interest until year 23—for the first 22 years of the mortgage in this example you would pay $565 000, but your mortgage balance would only reduce by $138 000.

To pay less to the bank you have to become mortgage-free faster, and this is where you need your cash surplus!

I wanted to pay my mortgage off faster, but I did not want to commit to a shorter term as I couldn't guarantee that I could afford the increased repayments, nor did I want my mortgage dictating the lifestyle I wanted to live. I still wanted to take a holiday and replace my car. I knew at some point I wanted a family. The thought of going down to one income definitely meant we couldn't afford fixed higher repayments. I wanted flexibility but I wasn't sure how to get this; flexibility typically comes at a higher—floating—interest rate. If you try to change your loan term, even if you leave the interest rate constant, it can still trigger a break cost. This is why I never recommend locking in a reduced term, as you never know if you might need to lengthen it.

THE POWER OF CALCULUS

How much flexibility did I need? How fast could I repay my debt?

Dr Jamie Sneddon, a calculus tutor at the University of Auckland, helped me to understand the calculus behind how banks structure debt, and how I needed to structure my mortgage to repay it as fast as my situation allowed, while living a lifestyle I could enjoy. With this tool I was able to strike the perfect balance.

The now-patented formula, which is eight pages long, makes one key assumption. That is, that you will have money left over at the end of the week, month or year to cover your one-off costs; for example, holidays, and that these funds can be channelled into repaying debt faster.

At the time I didn't have a cash surplus—credit cards were my buffer for random one-off costs and there were times when I couldn't repay my credit card in full. As it turned out, my husband and I were frittering close to $20 000 every year, spending more as our incomes increased. I don't know exactly where all the money went but I do own a lot of shoes! Once we had a general idea where the money was going we found $20 000 we could save—channel into our mortgage—without affecting our happiness and lifestyle. Without a payrise above inflation the result was that we would be mortgage-free in nine years and save $368 000 in interest costs. (In actual fact, we repaid our mortgage even faster than that because of payrises and the fact that we picked up momentum.)

The graph below shows our initial mortgage balance of $300 000 and the speed at which it was reducing. Sticking to the bank repayments, you can see we would have been mortgage-free in 30 years. Channelling our new-found surplus of $20 000 per annum, we were able to reduce the mortgage term to just nine years.

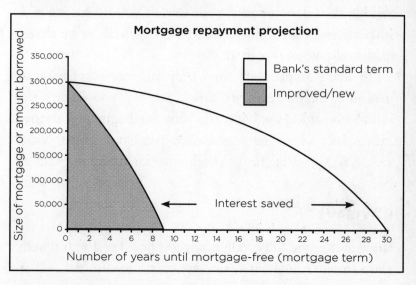

The Perfect Balance

Repaying your mortgage as fast as your lifestyle allows is usually the best strategy to grow wealth because the average guaranteed risk-free return on repaying your mortgage is 8 per cent after tax and inflation. I am often asked if it makes more sense to repay debt or save. It usually comes down to the numbers for return versus risk. For example, if you had a guaranteed risk-free return on an investment or term deposit of 12 per cent gross—8 per cent after tax—then saving would be a valid substitute to repaying debt. But in all likelihood it is unlikely such an investment exists—with the exception of KiwiSaver—so making debt repayment the preferred choice.

The key though is not to force money towards your mortgage. Instead, live a lifestyle you enjoy, capture the money left over, and channel any surplus towards the mortgage. If you do it correctly you will not feel like you are on a budget. And if it feels effortless, and you are seeing better results, then it becomes sustainable. If you do not have a sustainable cash surplus, then all energy needs to be channelled into fixing this first.

In the example above, not only are you debt-free in a maximum of nine years, you save money that you would have otherwise paid to the bank and your fixed outgoings drastically reduce when you become debt-free. Once this happens, saving and investing for your retirement is straightforward.

KIWISAVER

KiwiSaver—and any other superannuation fund where your employer matches your contribution—is one of the better forms of investments you can make, especially if you are starting out. This is because for every dollar of your income you invest, your employer is investing a dollar of theirs. These funds are pooled and invested in a fund of your choosing. Even if the fund has no growth, you have still made a 100 per cent return with minimal risk. KiwiSaver is not for everyone, but if you are not in KiwiSaver think about joining.

Some people are unable to afford KiwiSaver because they are sinking financially. This problem needs to be fixed before you ring-fence money for the future. There is no point worrying about retirement if you are going to be bankrupt tomorrow. Instead, put all energy into creating a cash surplus so you are in a position to benefit from KiwiSaver in the future.

If you are saving for your first home and have been in KiwiSaver for three years you can access your contributions and use these towards your deposit. If you have not been in KiwiSaver for three years and you want to buy a house, you may consider taking a contributions holiday in order to save the necessary deposit to allow you to get the house, before re-commencing contributions. See <www.kiwisaver. govt.nz> for more information.

Chapter 5

Investing

Once you have cleared your mortgage you can start to think about other forms of investing. You can invest in many areas, including more property, superannuation, term deposits, shares and businesses.

INVESTMENT PROPERTY

The most popular form of investment in New Zealand is property. It's not surprising it is popular—we are a DIY nation, we understand property, and it gets a better return than bank deposits. It is considered safer then the common alternative of shares. Once you own one property, it is easy to own a second, and then a third, due to your ability to leverage or access the equity in your properties.

Once you have enough equity in that first property—this usually means at least 20 per cent equity in your home—you'll find yourself in a position to approach the bank to borrow against it to buy another property. This is called leveraging—you might borrow 10 per cent against your home to use as the deposit for the investment property. You can rent out the second property, to help pay the mortgage on it.

If you buy the right property and structure the ownership

correctly, the investment property should be able to pay for itself. As the second property increases in value, you leverage off that to buy a third property, and so on. Provided the properties pay for themselves, over time you receive capital gains as they increase in value. All you have done is simply hold the property and maintained it. When you are ready, you sell a portion of your investment portfolio and take the profit. This has been regarded as an easy way to build wealth, and many people have done this successfully.

Although the idea is that the rent tenants pay will cover the mortgage, there is usually a shortfall. According to census data, the average rental yield is 5 per cent, with annual rent increases tracking close to inflation. Because the average interest rate is higher—at 8 per cent—most property investors have to 'top up' the mortgages to cover all the costs on their investment properties.

However, provided you have structured your investment correctly, for every dollar you put into the property you will receive up to 33 cents back in tax refunds at the end of each financial year. Topping up a property means it is giving you a negative cash-flow return, or the investment is 'negatively geared'.

As I mentioned earlier, many people believe that having a negatively geared property is a good thing because of the tax benefits, but this is not always correct. You are still paying $1 in costs to get that 33 cents back. It is usually best not to have spent the dollar in the first place. Having a property you have to 'top up' is only worthwhile if, over time, the increase in capital value is less than what you have spent 'topping it up'.

Many clients ask if their investment property is a good property. To be 'good' it needs to be increasing in value, and the cost of holding the property needs to be less than the overall gain made. It only makes sense to top up a property if it is expected that the capital gain over time is going to outweigh the amount of money you have spent topping it up.

It is important that you do the maths on this. Each property stands by its own merits.

A client purchased a property eight years ago for $220 000. At the time she required a 10 per cent deposit of $22 000. She borrowed the rest. The property is now worth $300 000, and if she was to sell it today, she is comfortable that she would receive its value in cash. It has increased $80 000. The property itself is negatively geared. This means that she has had to top it up every year by around $3000. She gets a tax refund of $1000 on this amount. So it costs her around $2000 per annum to hold the property. She has held it for eight years. This means she has spent around $16 000 to hold the property and keep it maintained. Overall she has made a net gain of $64 000 over the last eight years, or an average gain of $8000 every year. That seems pretty good. But we need to compare it against what would have happened if she had put her deposit of $22 000 into the bank and topped up that investment by $2000 each year, as she did the investment property. The average interest rate after tax and inflation is 1 per cent.

If she put the money in the bank for eight years, she would have earned $40 000 after adding $2000 per annum and the interest earned. Owning a property in this instance provides a better return and seems to be performing well. To establish whether a property is performing well, you need to compare it to other investments that carry similar levels of risk. This is when you compare the opportunity cost of the investment.

Each property must stand by its own merits and you need to work out the financial prospects for each property before buying it. If you are relying on capital gain, make sure the area you are buying in has good capital-gain prospects. If you want to buy an investment property but it will require huge cash injections each week to service the mortgage, make sure you can afford to make these payments.

While property has clear benefits, one frustration is that the capital gain is not linear—it doesn't increase in value consistently and smoothly every year. It gains according to where we are in the property cycle. If you are going to inconvenience yourself by becoming a landlord, you need to make sure that you can afford to hold onto the property for the next property cycle—historically it's a nine to ten year cycle. If you cannot do that there is no guarantee that you will get back the money you have invested in it should you need to sell it sooner than planned.

It is interesting to note that rental yields seem to more or less track inflation over time. In the world of property investing, houses are priced off their achievable rental yields assuming 100 per cent financing. To calculate this, simply take the annual rental yield for a property and divide it by the house price, and you have a measure of how 'expensive' a property actually is.

When working out how much a property is going to cost it is important that you use an average interest rate, as opposed to today's rate, which may be lower.

Remember, on average over ten years the interest rate is around 8 per cent. You need to use this as the interest rate to calculate how much the property is going to cost you, as it is likely that while you are waiting for property prices to increase, the interest rates will increase. I have a number of clients who have had to sell their investment property prematurely because they cannot afford to hold onto it during a higher-interest-rate environment.

TERM DEPOSITS

A term deposit is a money deposit at a bank that cannot be withdrawn for a fixed period of time or 'term' (unless a penalty is paid or interest is forfeited). When the term is over it can be withdrawn or it can be held for another term. Generally speaking, the longer you leave the money in the bank, the better the interest rate (yield) offered.

The rate of return is higher for a term deposit than a standard savings account because the bank is not obliged to return the money to you on demand. Instead the bank can take the money and invest it for a period of time (within the initial term), to gain higher returns than being on call.

Term deposits are typically provided by mainstream banks. They are typically low-risk, as we assume that the bank will not go bust and the government would step in if something went wrong. Term deposits are simple to set up and have very few conditions attached. That said, you should understand what the bank is using the funds for. Usually mainstream banks lend these funds under their general guidelines; for example, if they lend to a developer they might take first mortgage over the development.

The return on this type of product is generally lower than that of investments in riskier products like stocks or bonds.

DEBENTURES

Debentures are similar in concept to a term deposit in the sense that you are paid interest over a fixed period and you are supposed to receive your money back at the end of the term. However, unlike a term deposit they can vary in risk. Higher-risk debentures should be paying a higher rate of return, although this is not always the case, especially when the finance company wants to 'downplay' the real risk of the investment. The finance company is free to on-lend the funds, much like a bank, and typically they lend the funds to higher-risk activities. They have terms and conditions that highlight where you 'rank' if the finance company goes under, which means you might not get all your money back if the finance company backs a dodgy investment. Be aware that finance companies are usually smaller outfits than banks and they have limited resources if a development goes under.

The paperwork will always say if a debenture is secured or unsecured. An unsecured debenture is riskier than a secured debenture, but being secured is a bit misleading because if the finance company goes under, the 'security' can count for little.

BONDS

Bonds are a fixed-interest product. You hand over your deposit and collect a payment (interest/coupon). Governments, local bodies, state-owned corporations and corporates can all issue bonds. When you buy a bond you are, in effect, lending money to the organisation issuing the bond. In New Zealand, bonds are traded on the New Zealand Debt Market (NZDX).

Governments borrow from the market to fund their day-to-day operations from within their country or from a foreign source by issuing bonds. Foreign-currency government debt is also known as sovereign debt. If you invest in foreign government bonds, you need to understand what is happening in the country you are investing in because the quality of the bond you are buying is only as good as the country issuing the bond (i.e. taking your money). You should never lend to anyone who cannot afford to pay you back—whether the borrower is a friend, a company or a government, the same rule applies. Until recently it was assumed that governments of large, stable countries were a relatively low-risk proposition because, like mainstream banks, they have significant resources to call on to honour their debts. However, if the county is technically bankrupt (as has recently happened to Greece) there will be no money to pay anyone.

Bonds issued by councils, local bodies and state-owned utilities are considered slightly higher risk than a government bond, as they are one stage removed from the government's obligations.

Similarly, bonds issued by corporations can be safe

or risky depending on who is issuing them. For example, Whitcoulls is an example of a corporation that issued bonds during the GFC. When the bonds matured, they returned the investment to the bond-holders, but two months later the company went into receivership. In theory, corporate bonds are considered more risky than most, but this blanket assumption is misleading. Like any investment, the risk is relative. The risk with corporate bonds depends on who the corporation is, where it is and the timing of the bond issue. For example, New Zealand finance companies were great for a long period of time, but in the space of eighteen months—between 2008 and 2010—most of them stopped trading and defaulted on their obligations. On the other hand, if Apple was to issue bonds they would be one of the safest investments in the world.

If it is a good bond, you are first in line to be paid out, should the company go under. Some bonds have an expiry or maturity date when you will be paid out. Perpetual bonds do not have a maturity date so you pay once and receive coupons/interest at a set rate but the issuer is not obliged to return your money at any set point. The coupon rate can be reset periodically and this is the main weakness of a perpetual bond—it may be reset at an unfavourable rate. Then, if you tried to sell it, you might lose.

Like shares, bonds can be complicated and require detailed and impartial analysis of performance and comparisons to other investments. If you do not have the understanding or time to do this, but you still wish to invest in these types of investments, you should probably have someone manage your bond portfolio for you.

SHARES

When you buy a share, you become a shareholder of the company. You are buying an equity participation in the company and, in most instances, the company will pay you an annual dividend based on the number of shares you own. This dividend is your share of the company's profit. You buy and sell shares on exchanges. To buy and sell shares in New Zealand you have to go through a stockbroker—either a bank or a financial adviser and New Zealand shares are listed on the exchange New Zealand Exchange Limited (NZX).

Interestingly, shares in New Zealand and Australia return higher dividends than anywhere else in the world. However there is an inherent risk with shares because there is no guaranteed dividend and there is no guarantee that the shares will go up in value. With fixed-interest investments you have a promise. With shares you hand the money over and hope.

In theory the money you invest in shares is worth something, but only while someone else values the shares—they are only as good as the selling price when you come to sell them. The problem with this is that the value of your investment is dependent on other people's perception of its value, because that is what markets are based on, people's perception. Shares go up in value and they go down. The potential for gain is enormous. In 2003, Apple shares were $6 each and now they are over $400. On the other hand, the risk of loss can be high. But the risk of loss is limited to the investment made.

SUPERANNUATION FUNDS AND LIFE INSURANCE POLICIES

It is possible to have superannuation funds that you have established and contribute to. These funds have nothing to do with your work, or KiwiSaver. Much like KiwiSaver, you pay into a fund that is ring-fenced, for your retirement. This means that you cannot access the money invested until a certain age—maybe 50, 55, 60, or 65—depending on the specific policy.

Like any investment you need to ask yourself two questions about a superannuation fund:

- If I am contributing $1 to this investment every month, am I better to keep paying into the fund, or should I invest my dollar elsewhere?

- If possible should I cash in my policy, and apply the capital to another investment; for example, reducing my mortgage?

The answers to these questions will depend on how well the fund is actually performing and if an employer is making contributions into your fund. Unfortunately, it is likely that the monthly statements sent to you do not always clearly show fund performance. Often these statements simply indicate how much you will receive if you withdraw your funds at an attractive and imagined rate of return. The problem is they do not show the actual rate of return. In many cases, when I have investigated for my clients I have found that the return has been less than 1 per cent for years! If it is unlikely that the return is going to increase it might pay to 'cut your losses' and withdraw the funds to invest elsewhere.

Do your homework and always read your investment statements carefully. Has the investment increased in value? If so, what rate is the increase? Is there an unrelated return on your investment? If you are not sure, call the fund manager and keep talking until you understand exactly what is happening to your investment. If the statement omits key performance data, you can usually bet the fund is not performing well.

WHICH INVESTMENT IS BEST FOR YOU?

In deciding which investment is best for you, you need to ask yourself two questions:

- How much of my wealth do I want to put at risk?

- How much risk do I want to take?

You will not be able to answer these questions until you can establish what return you need to achieve from the money invested to achieve your financial goals.

To determine what risk is needed, you need to understand whether you are on track to achieve your financial goals with savings alone, whether you want to buy a first home or plan for retirement. If there is a shortfall, this will help you calculate the level of return you need in order to grow your wealth to a sufficient level, so that you are able to meet your goal.

It is important that you distinguish between your

tolerance for risk and your capacity for risk. For example, many retired couples had money invested in finance companies before the global financial collapse. They were getting a good return—interest rate—on the money invested. Unfortunately, a great number of those people who invested their money in the high-interest, high-risk investments could not afford to lose the capital they had invested. They have been left shaking their heads and asking why they exposed their hard-earned money to such risky investments. Sometimes the best investments are the ones you do not make. Follow Donald Trump's advice and only invest in products you understand and people you know you can trust.[17]

An important side note here: whether you trust the celebrity endorsing a product has no relevance. (Personally, I think it is unethical to have any celebrity endorse an investment or finance company unless they started it themselves or are one of the investors and have their investment disclosed.) Famous face or not, there's no good reason for investing your hard-earned money in something you do not understand. I've heard of so many people who have invested in finance companies and the like because of the face of the company's advertising campaign. And they have lost their money. It's sad, but these people took no precautions. They simply wrote out a cheque to someone they didn't know, for a product they didn't understand. In all likelihood the famous face probably didn't understand what they were representing either. But, I've said it before—the only person who will ever truly care about your money is you. Don't be stupid or reckless, and do not cry foul play when you yourself took no precautions. Stand up and take some responsibility for your investments, and invest on sound principles and the merits of each investment and how it will affect your longer-term goals.

WHOSE ADVICE SHOULD YOU SEEK?

A lot of advisers specialise in one field, and can give you good advice in that area, but their advice is given in isolation. They may give good investment advice, but not good financial advice as it relates to the nuances of your personal situation.

For example, to buy and sell shares in New Zealand you have to go through a stockbroker—either a bank or a financial adviser. Stockbrokers clip the ticket from both sides of the transaction.

A financial planner will take a look at your wider circumstances, and may do a good job managing your money to retirement, but may not know much about specific investments. They get around this by handing it to a fund manager who will manage the investments for them on your behalf. The fund manager, like the stockbroker, will clip the ticket on the funds invested, irrespective of results achieved. If financial management is a problem, they do not have the systems available to fix the problem.

An insurance adviser gives advice on insurance policies, but unless they are qualified to comment beyond that, it is best not to rely on further advice given. This is not so much a problem overall with the new regulations effective since 2011, but this is a relatively new feature. Accountants often say they are business advisers, but in a lot of instances they simply complete your tax return and add little value to the day-to-day running of your business.

Getting advice from the right people is critical to getting ahead, so work out what you need to know and who best can answer your questions.

RETIREMENT PLANNING

Quite simply, most people are not going to have enough money to pay for the sort of retirement they want. So you pay your taxes and believe that this should entitle you to a pension. Maybe it should. The point is immaterial if, by the time you retire, there is not enough money to pay pensions. Whining will not change this fact. With good planning for financial success you should be able to avoid a feeling of panic.

Remember, it's not just about the numbers. You need to understand how your emotions affect your money behaviour and, just as importantly, how money is treated within your personal relationships. (To find out more see 'Your money personality', page 14 and 'Personality combinations', page 19.)

Retirement planning is about taking your savings—the ten per cent you have at the end of each week, month or year—and making more money with it. Successful retirement planning will enable you to make enough money to fund a lifestyle you will enjoy well after you stop working.

A lot of Kiwis—too many—expect retirement to sort itself out. I am all for positive thinking—that 'she'll be right', 'can-do' attitude we identify as our positive, national characteristic. When it comes to money and retirement planning, however, you can dress things up however you want to, but if you are going backwards you are going backwards. If this is the case for you, the sooner you realise it the sooner you have a shot at bridging the gap between where you are now and where you need to be by the time you retire.

You can borrow for many things in life— your homes, cars, children's education or university fees—but you cannot borrow to pay for your retirement. To fund retirement, you need to have saved enough money to live the lifestyle you enjoy. There's a small correlation between your income and happiness but how much you will need to save will depend on the lifestyle you want. Let's keep it simple. You will need to ask yourself the following questions:

- How much do I need to spend to be happy with my lifestyle?

- Do I want to be able to travel when I retire? If so, how often, how far and how much will it cost?

- What one-off costs will I have after I retire?

- Do I intend to be mortgage-free when I retire?

- Do I plan to downsize my house around the time I retire?

- Do I have a superannuation policy? If so, how much am I likely to receive when I retire?

- Am I likely to get an inheritance?

Challenge your assumptions about the things you think you need and squeeze the frittered expenses to minimise the day-to-day costs of your lifestyle. Do it now! Remember financial success is not about how much you make, but how much you keep.

If you are not mortgage-free when you come to retire, consider downsizing your home so that your mortgage payments do not cause your retirement savings to haemorrhage.

Both downsizing your home and receiving an inheritance provide one-off income, but it can be a bit tricky to rely on these to save you because you do not have control over the amount provided or timing of them.

$$\text{Lifestyle costs} \times \text{Years living in reitirement} + \text{One-off costs} - \text{One-off cash injections} = \text{What your retirement will cost}$$

Once you have put some numbers around these things, we can work out what your retirement is going to cost. If the thought of putting numbers to these things is too hard for you, or you don't have time to work it out, enlist the help of an expert who is not trying to get you to invest in a product they are flogging.

Multiply this cost by the number of years you might reasonably expect to live after you retire. This will tell you how much you need to have saved before you reach retirement. Subtract what you have now, and the difference is what you need to save between now and retirement.

So what does this look like in practice? Here is a case study of a couple both aged 45. They have a combined income of $160 000, one child, a home worth $500 000 and a mortgage of $300 000, payable over 25 years. Their daughter is planning to go to university, but will take out a student loan to pay for her course. They both contribute 2 per cent of their income to KiwiSaver. They want to retire at 65 and they want to keep living their current lifestyle in retirement. They want to know if this is a realistic goal, or whether they need to get used to the idea of working for longer.

Before working with me they were spending all the money they earned. Now, they have a cash surplus of $25 000 per annum. They intend to replace their car every ten years, spending $10 000 to do so. They also intend to spend $15 000 on a holiday to Europe. As long as they continued to spend everything they earned, funding retirement was not possible. However, after we worked to create a cash surplus of $25 000 per annum and channelled the money into their mortgage, they were in a position to pay off their mortgage faster. Even with car replacements and the trip to Europe, you can see from the following graph that they should be mortgage-free in ten years. This will save them $215 000 of interest, which will be a much-needed injection for retirement.

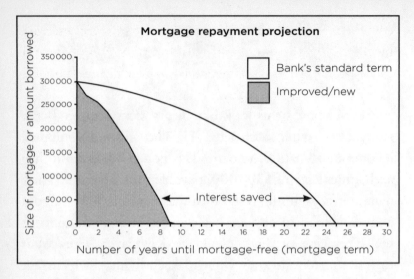

The white area on the graph above shows their current mortgage of $300 000 and the number of years before they will be mortgage-free if they stick to their current arrangement with the bank. However, by working to a plan they can create a cash surplus which allows them to repay the mortgage faster, shown by the grey area. While it is preferable to channel all funds into repaying your mortgage as fast as you can, one-off costs like car replacements and overseas holidays need to be funded from the cash surplus, which means in the year these larger one-off events occur, the mortgage will not reduce at the same rate as prior years. The graph above has a few bumps that indicate when money is being spent on other areas. Overall though, factoring in the things they want to plan for, they are still in a position to be mortgage-free in ten years, which is a fantastic result.

After ten years, or when they are mortgage-free if that is sooner, the money that was going to repay the mortgage can be saved. Their fixed mortgage payments previously cost them $25 000 per annum so their savings will increase by at least that amount. Instead of having $25 000 left over each year, in ten years' time, their cash surplus will double to $50 000—excluding payrises and bonuses.

If this surplus goes into a savings account, earning 1 per cent interest after tax and inflation they will be able to save approximately $480 000 before retirement. They could then access these savings, along with their KiwiSaver on retirement. These funds, coupled with the current pension, would allow them to maintain their current lifestyle until age 80, at which point they would need to downsize their home unless they have received a one-off windfall, such as an inheritance. It's also worth noting here that most people reduce their spending after they retire by up to as much as 30 per cent.

The usual goal is to be able to fund your retirement until you are 80, somehow. Some people need to buy and hold an investment property because the funds they have invested in the bank are not giving them the return they need to achieve their retirement goals.

The bridge between where you are now and where you want to be has to be quantified with a clear plan of attack put in place, otherwise you are not going to successfully sustain your lifestyle after you retire.

For some, buying and holding an investment property is enough to create the needed gain when they sell the property. For others selling the investment property is not the objective and they repay mortgage on an investment property to receive rental income in perpetuity. Provided their living costs are less than the rental income an investment property could fund your retirement nicely.

Chapter 6

Understanding your capability

*Continuous effort—not strength or intelligence—is the
key to unlocking our potential. — Winston Churchill*

No matter where you are starting from—whether you are
sinking, floating or flying—you need to have a plan and to
make a start.

MAKING A START

To make a start you must be honest about your finances.
You must understand what you own, and what you owe. You
need to know exactly how much you earn and what your
total income is, and what you spend your money on. If you
have no money left at the end of each pay cycle, ask yourself
these three questions:

- Why?

- Where is my money going?

- What can I do to change things and start saving?

Establish what costs you can cut back on and see if that
will be enough to create a cash surplus. If it is not, do more.
Sell assets, get a second job, but ensure you have money left
at the end of each month.

Sorting out your finances takes time. If you are time-poor get someone else to do it for you, but make sure you are both accountable for results.

As an opera singer, Beverly Sills knew all about hard work when she said, 'There are no shortcuts to any place worth going.' The same is true for you—the harder you work, the luckier you will become.

In order to refine your strategy for any journey you undertake, including managing your money, you need to understand the exact distance that needs to be covered, what terrain you are likely to encounter and the best vehicle for your journey.

In terms of decisions around money before you begin a journey, ask yourself the following four questions:

- Where am I financially?

- What potential do I have?

- Where do I want to be?

- What is standing in my way?

THE STARTING POINT

Money troubles and denial typically go hand in hand—denial is when you simply refuse to recognise or acknowledge a situation. This refusal to look at a situation often causes people to create serious financial issues for themselves. For example, when your bank statement comes in do you open it or do you throw it in a pile to look at later? Do you even know how much money is in your bank account? When was the last time you deposited money into your bank account, not including your pay? Do you even know how much you are paid?

If you can't answer these questions you are either hands-off with your finances or in denial about your financial situation. If you are to start to make progress towards your financial goals, you need to be honest. Leaving everything to your spouse is not delegation; it is shirking your own responsibility. Successful delegation means you still have a handle on things, you know what is happening and why, and could step in at any point. While finances are often left to one spouse to manage, if you are not on the same page your progress will be uneventful, if there is any progress at all. Further, the spouse who is 'carrying the can' often feels stressed or frustrated at the lack of buy-in, leading to conflict or dissatisfaction in the relationship. Articulating your personal relationship with money and the role of money in your relationship can be stressful for some people, and I have to say some clients cry the first time they meet with me.

The first time that a client sees me, we set about diagnosing where they are at financially. As part of this process we want to ascertain if they are naturally on track to achieve their financial goals. If clients are on track to achieve their financial goals, we spend time establishing if they can reach their goals faster, by doing certain things differently. If they aren't, we want to find what might be standing in their way, and what they could be doing differently to get a different outcome. For most people it is a pretty full-on, but ultimately rewarding, experience.

It is compulsory that both partners in a relationship be in attendance for this meeting as it is important for partners to go through this process together—I won't work with them otherwise. This is because, in my experience, any spouse not willing to attend this first meeting is usually a key reason for the couple's current financial position, so trying to fix the financial landscape without their engagement is like trying to drive a car with a flat tyre. No matter how much energy is put into steering the vehicle, you will continue to be pulled in the wrong direction.

Strangely, at least 10 per cent of new clients are desperate to attend this first meeting by themselves. I have heard all of the reasons you could possibly imagine and then some, including 'I'm the problem, not my spouse', 'My partner has no idea of where things are at—they don't manage the money' and 'He/she doesn't listen to me anyway'. If you are in a relationship both you and your partner have contributed to your financial situation. And you both need to develop new life skills to correct this situation. If your partner has no idea where things are at, it is time they stood up and started paying attention. Everyone has a moral and social responsibility to know how they are doing financially. Burying your head in the sand is no longer good enough.

I completely understand that it can seem daunting and you may have tried to change things but have gotten nowhere—but often, continuing with the status quo is not an option.

Having both spouses at the first meeting will give them both a new understanding of their partner and what makes them tick financially. Often, people incorrectly assume that the spender in the relationship is responsible for their demise, or lack of progress, but this is only one determining factor. Often the person who is tight on a day-to-day basis decides when they do want to buy something that they will spend 'whatever is needed' to get what they want. Usually it is the spending on big items that creates a problem—not the occasional little treats.

I once had a man visit for a first meeting without his wife because they had a sick child. This was the first time he had truly confronted the state of his finances and he was embarrassed. He earned more than $400000 per annum and was in a very high-profile job. I emailed a summary of the meeting to the household's joint email address and he called me back within five minutes of receiving the email. He asked me to omit certain details of their financial situation from my original email because he didn't want his wife to know the cold hard truth of their situation.

My reply was, 'You have successfully managed to get your household finances into a mess without your wife being any the wiser. You have had your turn and it didn't work. If you want to fix this situation, you need to do what I say, and that means everything out on the table. Because we all need to be on our game to fix your situation.'

In all honesty I was just as frustrated with his wife, who had happily buried her head in the sand and taken a 'hands-off' approach to her finances and theirs, but that was beside the point. Both spouses need to be on the same page otherwise they are going to have issues.

I did not resend an amended version of my original email. I did, however, send a follow-up email that said no matter how dire their situation seemed it could be fixed, provided they were prepared to do whatever was necessary. If they were, they could be sure of a positive outcome.

Although I can understand why people might hesitate to share all the information with their spouses, especially when it looks bad for them, it is a pretty short-sighted approach. Everything comes out in the wash in the end.

Omitting financial details is not uncommon for many couples. Somewhere between 5 and 10 per cent of my clients find out information about their joint finances they were not previously privy to (possibly because they didn't care to ask) at their first meeting with me. This is consistent with data from the US that has showed that 9 per cent of spouses are prepared to keep silent about aspects of their financial situation because knowing about the issue would worry their partner.[18] (You don't say.) Seven per cent of respondents said they'd keep it secret because telling would damage their relationship. One has to ask—if in knowing the truth the relationship might be damaged, doesn't that imply it already is?

Whether you know all the details about your current financial position or not is irrelevant before starting this exercise. The objective is to know your position *after* you have completed the exercise. Fill in the Financial assessment template in Appendix III to get a snapshot of your financial position or current status.

Here is the series of questions I ask new clients to get a snapshot of their financial position:

- What are your tradeable assets?

- What are your liabilities, including your student loan?

- Do you have credit card debt?

- Do you clear your credit card every time payment is due?

- Are you contributing to KiwiSaver?
  — If so, at what rate?

- Do you have savings?
  — If so, how much?
  — If not, why not?

- What does your situation feel like?
  — Do you feel in control of your money?
  — Do you feel that you are getting ahead?

- If you lost your job tomorrow, what would happen to you?

- Do you have children?
  — If so, how many and how old are they?
  — If not, do you want children?

- Do you owe tax?

- Do you own investment properties?
  — If so, are the properties negatively geared or does the rent received cover the mortgage and rates?

- Is your employment secure?
  — Have you reached your income potential?
  — Are you likely to receive payrises or bonuses?

— How much do you get paid in the hand—hitting the bank account—every week, fortnight, or month?

- Are you self-employed?
  — Do you draw a regular wage?
  — Can you put costs through the business?
  — Do your financial statements show income paid to you?
  — Are you paid cash or with contras?
  — Who manages the money?
  — Do you have to juggle things each week?

- Do you own your own property in a trust?
  — If not, why not?

- Who manages the money in your relationship?
  — Why?
  — Are you both engaged with your finances?

- Do you find it easier to spend or save?

- What are your non-negotiable costs?
  — Do you have to go on a family holiday each year?
  — Do you want your kids to have swimming lessons?
  — Do you need to buy a flat white every day?

- Do you think you fritter your money?

- How many bank accounts do you have and how does money flow between them?

The answers to these questions help paint a picture of their current location and what obstacles or attitudes are holding them back. Basically, I need new clients to tell me their stories so I can incorporate everything I notice into a workable financial plan for them. All these points need to be considered and weighted for each situation. Once we all know where they are, they need to understand how they got to that point. Is it because they have frittered money, paid more tax than necessary, overused their credit card(s), made poor financial decisions in the past, or simply that they need a good plan to stick to? If they've lacked motivation in the past what will motivate them now? (See Chapter 1 for more on money personalities, common obstacles and money traps.)

> **Don't judge your spouse's non-negotiables.
> It will end in tears.**

Understanding the nuances of each unique situation is critical to developing a realistic plan to help individuals and partners to achieve the perfect balance. All these questions need to be answered honestly before I even begin to look at numbers, such as income versus spending. Before I consider people's actual spending I need to know how it feels for them on a day-to-day basis.

MAKING A PLAN

I work with clients for four weeks preparing a plan. A plan has to be fluid enough to absorb life's curve balls and unexpected expenses, and make it possible to get ahead when windfalls happen. Most of all, a plan has to be achievable if it is going to build momentum.

Ironically, most people do not know what they are capable of. Looking at bank statements does not define what you could do—it simply tells you what you have done. I am reluctant to be dictated to about your potential by your bank statements, which is reassuring for many of my clients who are embarrassed by the state of their spending. In developing a plan with clients, we start with a best guess of what they think they can achieve. We need to get all the ducks lined up so that positive results are evident as soon as the plan is put in place. Basically every obstacle that has previously stood in their way is tidied up or restructured in the first four weeks of working with a client, so that the odds of success are well and truly tipped in their favour.

In addressing obstacles, the best approach is to work out a spending plan to capture the money that had been previously frittered, restructure bank accounts so that money cannot be inadvertently spent so easily, cancel credit cards or restructure mortgages or business affairs to minimise tax payments going forward. Every decision from this point on is going to have an impact that can be seen and felt.

After the first four weeks, often after I have restructured a client's mortgage and bank accounts, they are in a position to start testing the budget. They then have to draw a line in the sand and suck it up. After the month's preparation, every client is chomping at the bit to get started. Most also start off with some hesitancy. But we're then at the business end of the equation where results need to be achieved and it needs to be established if the plan is doable. To see if the plan is possible we test it, and the assumptions it is built upon, for twelve weeks. Then, together, we measure progress and refine the plan to better reflect the day-to-day needs of the client. Twelve weeks is short enough for anyone to commit to, while being a sufficient length of time in which to see a result.

Within every plan it is important you have enough money to do the things that are important to you, otherwise the plan won't work. Once a client is comfortable that the plan—budget—is achievable, we get together and I explain how things need to work on a day-to-day basis. This is quite detailed, including how much money the client needs to spend on a weekly basis to cover weekly costs, such as groceries, takeaways, coffees and petrol. This money is put into a separate account with a weekly automatic payment. They can manage this money as they see fit. I encourage people to use cash, but it is up to my clients to take responsibility to ensure that the money covers their weekly costs. If the money runs out, it runs out, and they need to wait until the next week before it is topped up again.

Bills, such as electricity, phone and internet, rates, and Sky TV, are paid from a separate account to avoid confusing fixed costs with weekly, more discretionary expenses.

For the next twelve weeks we track actual spending to the budget, to establish whether the plan is, in fact, sustainable. The goal is for the client to reach the end of the twelve-week period with an awareness of every dollar they have spent, but not to the point they feel deprived. If they can achieve this, the budget is working and we can all have confidence that it should continue to work. It is important that progress is tracked to the dollar. If you should have saved $2000 in the first twelve weeks, then this saving needs to be visible.

Consideration needs to be given to any unforeseen, unusual expenses or changes in the next quarter and new targets are set. Then we repeat the process of tracking and measuring actual results to forecasted capability after another twelve-week period. If clients are on track after twelve weeks, but their situation feels too 'tight', tweaks are made to the budget to ease the pressure on spending because if things are feeling tight there is a likelihood that clients will stray from their plan.

For most people, after the first twelve weeks the results speak for themselves. Sure, the plan may need some refinement, but if one can see the result of their efforts, money is no longer a misunderstood phenomenon; instead, it's something that is understood. Money makes friends with those who stick to the rules, and laughs at those who do not. If you stick to the rules, you will get the result, guaranteed.

My job at this point is to keep my clients on track, refine the plan, keep their emotion removed from the process and, at times, to force the results until the client's confidence grows enough to build momentum. I am accountable to the results as much as they are because I believe that if the emotion is removed, the results are sure to follow.

If you are not working with a financial personal trainer, then to keep motivated you need to ensure you are achieving your targets. Set goals, and know what you are capable of and what is not possible. Don't make things too tight. Allow for treats. Understand the timing of one-off costs and how they are going to affect the cash flow. Some months are going to be tighter than others due to when big bills are paid, so plot this and get your head around it. You feel in control when your money progress is in line with what you expect.

WHERE DO YOU WANT TO BE?

Your financial destination is where you want to be and it includes what you want to achieve along the way. Your destination is broken down into short-, medium- and long-term goals that mark the road to your success.

Along the way to a comfortable retirement you may have other more specific goals. Although each person's path may vary, you must keep checking your progress against your road map to ensure you remain on track overall. As science fiction writer Robert Heinlein once said, in the absence of clearly defined goals people become strangely loyal to performing daily acts of trivia; or, to paraphrase the writer Johann Wolfgang von Goethe, it is not enough to take steps that may, some day, lead to a goal—each step must in itself be a goal and a step in the right direction. Make every step count so that you can achieve the perfect balance, getting ahead as fast as your circumstances allow.

SETTING GOALS

Because a lot of people are intimidated by money, they fail to set goals for themselves and never change their financial outlook.

When encouraging my clients to set goals, or to list the things they want to achieve, I ask them to list goals for the next twelve months, the next two to five years and beyond. The most common goals are listed below.

Short term—next 12 months	Medium term—next 2–5 years	Long term—next 10+ years
Feel in control of my finances	Replace my car in X years, spending $X	Be mortgage-fee
Develop a plan	Renovate my property, spending $X	Save for retirement
Repay short-term and credit card debt	Take a holiday in X years, spending $X	Complete retirement planning
Pay off my mortgage faster	Buy an investment property	Buy an investment property
Stop living payday to payday	Protect my wealth	Buy a holiday home
Remove money worries from my relationship	Start a family	Buy a boat
Live a lifestyle I enjoy	Pay for a wedding	Take at least six months off work
Know my longer-term goals are in hand		
Buy a property		
Start a family, and go down to one income		
Refinance		

With each client we ensure that we achieve their immediate goals over the first twelve months and then refine their plan, where necessary, to achieve their medium- and long-term goals faster. The sooner all your goals are achieved the sooner you can stop working!

STRATEGIES FOR SUCCESS

These simple tricks will help you keep on track to your financial goals:

- Separate out your weekly costs from all other costs.

- Always use cash or eftpos—avoid credit cards or finance options, as they usually make it easier to spend more and will attract interest penalties.

- Set a budget.

- Track your spending.

- Tweak your budget to make it sustainable.

- Measure your results.

- Have a budget fluid enough to absorb curve balls and the timing difference of purchases.

- Celebrate progress!

CASE STUDY 1—HIGH DEBTS, NO PROPERTY

Natalie came to me at the age of 28 with high debts and no property. She was on a salary of $65 000 per annum (before tax), and had a $47 000 debt from spending on herself. Natalie thought she had a great relationship with her personal banker because she could call her up and ask for an extension on her credit card or personal loan and it would be available for access within 24 hours.

She struggled to repay her debts so consolidated and refinanced to another bank, repeating this process twice. Each time she refinanced for slightly more and kept on spending. Her main vice was clothing—she always looked good, but she was going backwards.

She was given a stark reality check when she finally went to a budget adviser and they told her to declare herself bankrupt. She called me and wanted to know what to do. We met and worked through her spending. For some people, bankruptcy is a legitimate option, although it is not usually the only option. Natalie wanted to repay her debts—she felt strongly about them being her responsibility. She didn't want to hide from the consequences of her actions, but she didn't have the tools to address the problem.

We listed all her expenses and debts. At a push, we could clear her debts within eighteen months if she was prepared to commit to a plan. The plan was tight and required very close monitoring to ensure she was making the best possible progress for her circumstances. It was important for her to see results quickly, otherwise she would lose momentum. She needed support, too, because she did not have the skills to achieve the result on her own.

After listing every creditor, we estimated how much she could afford to repay. She then contacted every creditor, explained her situation and started repayments. Not once did she default—she was ready and determined to sort things out once and for all. As debts were repaid, she had slightly more money to pay towards the remaining creditors. Whenever a debt was repaid, she contacted the remaining creditors, and advised them she could afford to pay them a higher rate. She kept this up for six months. She became known as the girl who knows what to do, and does what she says she is going to do. Instead of being a bad debtor, her creditors were viewing her more favourably.

When it came to her clothing addiction, I asked Natalie to commit to a strict budget for twelve weeks, to allow us to get some runs on the board. We slashed her shopping budget during this time and I asked her to make do with her existing wardrobe, or massage other costs down to allow her to spend money on clothes if she needed to. She stuck to the plan though. She was determined. And when she saw the result after twelve weeks she was motivated to keep going (although I did increase her clothing budget after that, as I didn't want her to fall off the wagon and have a clothing binge attack).

Over the first twelve months her income increased slightly and her contract changed to receive commission payments. She asked me what she should do when she received her first commission payment. I told her to call her creditors and ask what they would accept as a full and final payment of their account. Surprisingly, one of her last creditors to whom she owed $20 000 accepted $10 000 as full and final repayment of their account!

Just fifteen months from meeting and working with me Natalie was debt-free and in control of her financial destiny. Now, she is saving for a house.

CASE STUDY 2—ASSET-RICH, CASH-FLOW POOR

Tom and Donald were both 43 years old when they first came to me. Tom is a company director and Donald is a teacher. Their annual combined income from salaries was $200 000. Their total debt was $550 000. They owned their home and two investment properties—one of the properties was leaky.

They were running two separate 'money lives'—Tom is more of a saver and Donald is more of a 'save up to buy' personality. Donald would save hard, but always with the intention of spending all his savings. As can happen, things became quite tense in their relationship because of money issues—they never seemed to have quite enough and were slowing resenting their mortgage mountain.

They understood they needed money to reach their aims in life, but they did not understand how to use money well. They had read all the get-rich and invest-in-property books and dived into buying their first rental property in 2000. They felt they were doing the right thing—according to the books, at least—but there was just never enough money to get on top of the large mortgage, household bills and credit card bills. Even though they were experiencing high levels of stress, they bought their home in 2006 and for the next three years could not get ahead.

Some might say they were asset-rich, but they were paying 'interest only' on all mortgages and felt the assets weren't really theirs—they were owned by the bank.

They received their reality check in 2009 when they discovered the first rental property they had bought had leaky-building syndrome and the repair bill could be as much as $150 000 that would need to be paid over the next five years. Who would lend them that money? How could they afford to pay interest on an even larger mortgage?

They had also just lost some savings in a collapsed finance company so their money issues were causing them more stress than ever. This is when they called me.

They were making no traction on their interest-only mortgages. I worked through a plan and discussed the implications with them.

Essentially, they were spending too much on their day-to-day costs, they were not doing everything they could to minimise their tax liability and they had no cohesion in their finances or financial goals. They had been frittering a lot of money—early assessments indicated they had been frittering over $40000 per annum. Initially they had $550000 of debt that was going to take them at least 30 years to repay. I say 'at least 30 years' as one of the mortgages was interest only, and they felt that they were struggling to keep up with their current mortgage payments, so the likelihood of paying their mortgage faster was not viable until there was money left over.

The following graph shows what could be achieved when all their obstacles were systematically addressed and a workable plan was created. Initially a graph like this is a projection. My role is to make the graph real, so that over time we plot our progress against the graph to ensure we are on track. Remember, if we remove emotion, the projected mortgage graph is a mathematical certainty.

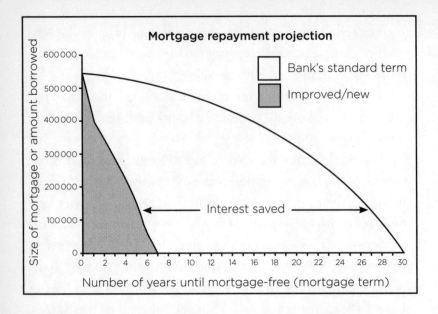

First projections suggested that they could repay all their debt in less than eight years, even after factoring in holidays and car replacements. A key part of optimising their financial position involved the following steps:

- They have only one credit card and pay off the full amount owing whenever it is due.

- They only ever use cash—in their case they chose to use eftpos—for petrol, groceries and meals out.

After eighteen months, they had cleared their hire-purchase debt, cleared their credit card debt and paid $155 000 principal off their mortgage. Most of the accelerated mortgage payments were the result of new savings they accrued by sticking to their new budget program, coupled with a slightly improved tax position. Money was now left over at the end of the week and that surplus, although quite small to start, consistently built over the course of time and was systematically applied to the mortgage.

Together they have changed the way they use and manage their money. Not only are their finances in a better shape, they now also have a family trust, decent wills, affordable life insurance and a day-to-day budget, plus their bills are all budgeted for and paid automatically each month.

And, it gets even better. In the past eighteen months they have enjoyed two overseas trips—one to California and one to Europe—that they've budgeted and paid for as they went. They still can't quite believe how they did this with seemingly little money stress!

Most importantly, they are $2236 ahead of their scheduled progress, which means they are on track to repay the mortgage sooner than the eight years initially projected. It is one thing to project an outcome—it is quite another to monitor progress and be accountable to achieving the projection. I still meet with them every twelve weeks to refine their plan, make allowances for new expenses and keep them motivated and on track.

They were initially nervous about giving up their freedom to spend money how and when they wanted. Now that they have learned how to create a budget and stick to it, they have also learned that the key to busting a mortgage is to fast-track how you pay off the principal. The interest rate is a cost for having the mortgage but, to be honest, the actual interest rate you are paying is not that important. It is more important how quickly you can pay off the principal.

Tom and Donald are no longer afraid of money or budgeting. They still love to spend but they factor this into their plan, so there is no guilt attached. Money is no longer a key issue in their relationship and they no longer run separate money lives. They actually work together better as a couple now with a set budget and defined money goals.

Reducing debt as fast as possible is the most beneficial and effective way to reducing stress. Above all, it allows you more choice about how you live your life.

> **Behaviour change is not so hard when you follow the right process and see results quickly.**

CASE STUDY 3—GOOD INCOME, BIG MORTGAGE, NO PROGRESS

Jody and Peter were both aged 39 and married with one seven-year-old child when they first came to me. Jody is employed as a solicitor and Peter is a communications consultant. Their combined before-tax income was $250 000 per annum.

They owned a house valued at $850 000 and had a mortgage of $650 000 that they were on track to pay off over 30 years. The mortgage payments left them feeling they didn't have any spare money—when there was an emergency, or they wanted a holiday, they'd always have to use credit to pay for it. Money was a constant source of stress. Although they could pay their bills and get by, they weren't getting ahead in paying off their mortgage—I think they'd become a bit defeatist about it.

They both wanted more balance in their lives and, if possible, to be able to work less. That simply wasn't a possibility with the size of their debt. They realised that if they didn't sort out their financial situation and reduce the debt they wouldn't have any options and may not be able to take up interesting opportunities that came their way.

There was some resentment on both sides in terms of how they each dealt with money. Despite agreeing to budgets they both kept on overspending. It was apparent that unless they did something drastic, their situation wasn't going to change.

Peter wanted to start working for himself, but he had no idea what his earning capacity would be. Their initial objective was to ensure he was earning a similar income to when he was an employee. Jody described herself as irresponsible with money although she came from a family of good savers. Her father had lost all hope in her being able to sort her situation out and told her to call me. He only hoped Jody and Peter might listen to someone they weren't personally involved with—much like people with a personal trainer at the gym.

When I met them they were on track to pay off their $650 000 mortgage in the allocated 30 years. Instead of spending because they could, we worked on a budget that allowed them to do the important things they wanted to spend money on. All remaining funds were captured and applied to the mortgage with the result being paying the mortgage off in fourteen years, after allowing for an annual family holiday and car replacements.

Our initial assessment suggested that they could repay their debt in less than fourteen years without any payrises or bonuses, while continuing to live a lifestyle they could enjoy. The initial projections also did not include allowances for the momentum that would pick up as they started to repay their debt faster.

Jody and Peter took to their budget like ducks to water. After two years, they have reduced their mortgage by over 30 per cent. They have stuck to their spending plan since and earned significantly more than forecasted. Before they had a plan, additional earnings would just be spent; now that money is captured and consciously allocated to reducing debt or buying things they want. Because their spending plan recognises everything they want to spend money on, when their income increases they don't need to spend more—they already have what they want. Having the plan has meant that they haven't frittered away the extra income.

Because they've also prioritised what's important to them, including a family holiday at least once a year, they've managed to have money for the things they want *and* been able to pay their bills without giving them a second thought. Best of all, they've got ahead in their goal to be mortgage-free. Having an earnings target has been very motivating for Peter. Being in his own business has given him an incentive to work hard, as he can see a direct impact from the effort he puts in.

Jody and Peter have learned that you can waste an awful amount of money on stuff that just doesn't really matter. It's the small things that can add up and after the first twelve weeks they looked back and said, 'Did we really spend

$4000 last year on coffee? That could be an extra holiday for the family or a new racing bike!'

The compounding results of the last two years mean that Jody and Peter have made up a lot of ground. Projections indicate that if they keep this momentum going they will be mortgage-free in five years, so they will have in fact halved the original time projected of fourteen years, and be repaid in just over an eighth of the time originally set up with the bank.

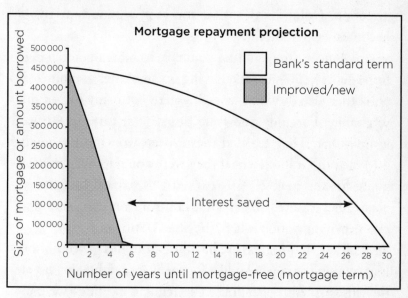

They feel in control of their finances and less stressed, and they no longer argue about money. Although they have achieved a lot already, it can be hard to be stay motivated simply to eliminate a mortgage—it's important to have some rewards along the way. They remain $15 000 ahead of schedule. If this momentum continues their mortgage can be repaid in around three years.

Jody would happily spend more money on clothes and eating out than is allowed in the quarterly budget. If they are ahead of target, Jody gets a one-off clothing allowance over and above what's set out in her budget. Two years into the planning I have asked them to think about something as a family they want to do that is outside of their current plan. This is to help keep them focused on what's important so that they continue the momentum they've built to date. Building in treats will keep them heading in the right direction. Going hard out for too long without any treats becomes wearisome.

Like most things in life, you have to be ready to change to be successful—just like giving up smoking, gambling or any other vice. It won't work if you're not ready to commit to change. For Jody and Peter, looking at turning 40 was a milestone. They realised they'd been working for nearly 20 years and it looked as if they were going to have to keep going for the next 20–30 years just to pay off their mortgage. They wanted to get some control over their situation and get in a position where they had options.

The keys to progress are having a clear idea of your priorities, making sure you budget for them, and tightening up on the miscellaneous spending. The regular meetings we continue to have to make them accountable, keep them enthused and on track to continue meeting their financial goals.

CASE STUDY 4—BUYING A HOUSE

Roger and Renee were aged 31 and 29 respectively and living in a de facto relationship when they first came to me.

Their combined after-tax income was $95 000 per annum. They had savings of $20 000 and, although they used credit cards to pay for their lifestyle, the bills were all paid in full each month.

They wanted to buy a house and had some money for a deposit but not quite enough to enter the housing market. As a result they had started spending all their income each month and felt ambivalent towards money.

Renee was the higher earner of the couple, and she was also the spender. By nature, Roger was a saver. They both wanted to become self-employed, but felt that this was not possible because of the likely financial impact on them. Roger accepted that because he earned significantly less than Renee he didn't have a right to question her spending. He felt disempowered as a result.

They wanted a house, but they did not know what they needed to do to actually get the house they wanted or how long it would take. They were fearful that buying a house would mean their lifestyle would be significantly and detrimentally impacted. After our first meeting, we identified $30 000 per annum that was being spent that needn't be. People earning a good income are known to spend because they have no reason not to. However, they soon learned they could live a lifestyle they enjoyed without that money being frittered. Over the course of the first six months they saved a further $15 000 and started looking for property.

After a couple of months of what seemed endless searching and attending challenging auctions they hadn't managed to buy a property and became despondent. They lost their focus and decided a trip to New York was just what they needed, so off they went and spent half their house deposit. They loved their trip but on their return realised they still wanted a house!

After that setback we reset the plan. It is important that what has been done is done—don't bother focusing on what you cannot undo. So often in relationships people feel aggrieved by their spouse's behaviour and focus on this, but I see little point to this. Instead, focus on what you can change and make up the ground lost. Six months later, with concerted effort and a payrise of $15 000, they were further ahead than when they left for New York. They purchased their first home for $320 000. They renovated and refurbished it, but the costs had been factored in right at the beginning so there were no financial surprises. When they announced they were getting married the cost of their wedding was factored into the plan, too, including the cost of a honeymoon to Thailand.

Roger is now self-employed. Before this transition, they worked to build sufficient headway on their mortgage to mitigate set-up costs and loss of income while he began to build his business. They optimised their mortgage by restructuring it to allow them to get ahead as fast as their new circumstances would allow while they continued to live a lifestyle they enjoy. Now, a snapshot of their mortgage structure shows they will be mortgage-free in six years—assuming no children.

A correctly structured mortgage, coupled with a fluid plan, allows you to access your equity as you need it, but still ensures your long-term picture remains rosy.

Remember, a successful plan is about stretching you to your full potential and adjusting to changes in circumstances. If you are waiting for the perfect time to start a plan, it will never come—financial stability is earned, not inherited, and the sooner you make a start the sooner it will be assured.

> **Mortgages and plans must never be static.**

When Roger and Renee finally purchased their house their lifestyle did not change; we simply replaced rent with mortgage payments and added in costs specifically related to property ownership. Because they had worked on their spending for some time they knew exactly what they needed to spend to have a lifestyle they liked. Without changing their discretionary spending, we simply channelled the surplus funds into repaying their mortgage faster. Initial projections suggest that they will be mortgage-free in around six years. This result is without relying on any payrises, just living as they have done. They are twelve months into their mortgage life and are $1500 ahead of where they needed to be at the end of year one to hold the projection true. If they keep this momentum up, they may be able to be debt-free in five years, or they can settle for six years and put the $1500 towards their next New York trip.

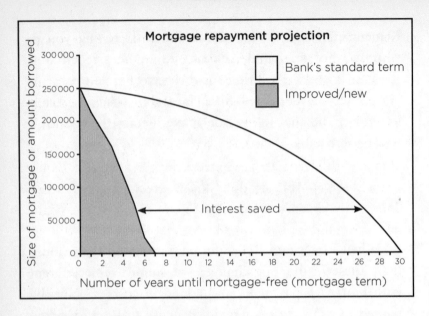

Mortgage repayment projection

- Bank's standard term
- Improved/new

Size of mortgage or amount borrowed

Number of years until mortgage-free (mortgage term)

Interest saved

CASE STUDY 5—TURNING 50

Louise and Billy were aged 50 and 52 respectively with a combined after-tax income of $98 000 when they first came to me. They were contributing to their employers' superannuation schemes at 4 per cent and these contributions were being matched by their employers. Their home was worth $330 000 and they were partway through a renovation with a further $20 000 to spend. They had a $224 000 mortgage. They also had other debts, which included a $20 000 loan to purchase their boat.

They said their situation was stagnant, but I would describe it as 'about to sink'. Their annual cash surplus was $10 000 but this was a false reading because they had $20 000 in consumer debt. They had a revolving credit mortgage—a recipe for disaster as it disguises people's lack of financial progress. A properly structured mortgage can be optimised so that it becomes another tool to help you get ahead as fast as your circumstances allow.

Louise and Billy both enjoyed gambling, smoking and drinking. They felt they worked hard and should be able to play hard. And play hard they did. Nonetheless, the fact that their goals seemed unattainable was dragging them both down. Billy desperately wanted a bigger boat and Louise wanted the renovations done and wanted help to get set up financially for their retirement, and to lend a financial hand to their children. None of this seemed likely. They did not feel in control and they did not understand how their mortgage worked. Instead, they continued to hope that going to work every day would provide them with a comfortable retirement.

After our first meeting our assessment showed their mortgage would not be repaid by retirement age, nor would there be any additional money to fund retirement. A bigger boat was certainly not possible. They had no inclination to change their lifestyle, so any plan would need to factor in gambling, smoking and drinking. The best plans make allowances for natural tendencies.

Their mortgage rate was high given the type of property they owned and because of how their bank had structured it. We were able to refinance them to another bank that viewed their property more favourably, reducing the interest rate and allowing a much-needed top-up to clear their debts and fund the last of the renovations. You could say they went backwards to get ahead, but time was not on their side—their retirement was less than fifteen years away.

If Louise and Billy kept doing what they had been doing

they would be mortgage-free in 20 years, but would still be feeling weighed down by their finances and not making any additional progress towards helping their family. After factoring in their goals and working backwards to establish what needed to be adjusted, we were able to build a plan that not only had their mortgage repaid in seven years, it also allowed for the bigger boat and opened the door for them to have the choice to retire at 62 (and they don't have to give up their vices).

Three years later they had completed their renovations and bought the bigger boat. They are $3300 ahead of schedule, and projecting forward at that rate of progress they will be mortgage-free in less than three years, which is much better than what was initially projected. After that the mortgage-payment money can be saved, too, putting them further head of their plan. If they continue to stick to this plan until they are aged 62, they will be able to fund their retirement until they are 81—assuming they receive a government pension at age 65. If they get a payrise above inflation during this period, they could extend the time over which they could fund their lifestyle in retirement or even decide to retire sooner.

As a further step, Louise and Billy have decided to acquire an investment property for their children to live in. The children will pay market rent, and this will be sufficient to cover the mortgage, so Louise and Billy are not 'topping up' the property. However, the main objective of this purchase is to make a capital gain on the property, from which the entire family will benefit in the long term. This is a great example of using family resources to everyone's advantage.

CASE STUDY 6—TURNING 60

Doris had just turned 60 and was single (having been wid-owed three years before) with two adult children, when she first came to me. She worked as a human resources adviser and had a before-tax salary of $70 000 per annum. She had just started contributing to KiwiSaver at a rate of 2 per cent. She had a stroke approximately twelve months before com-ing to see me.

She owned a property worth $710 000, next to her daughter's property. She had a $250 000 mortgage. There was a large home and a minor dwelling on her property, and Doris lived in the minor dwelling and rented out the main house for $605 per week.

The mortgage on her property had seventeen years to run. She thought she was operating her finances to break even. However, if she had factored in the biennial trips overseas she enjoyed she would have seen that she was going backwards. Because of the support she got from her daughter living next door she did not want to move, nor did she want to give up her overseas travel. She was happy to work for another eight years.

She got a reality check when she had the stroke. At the time her primary focus was on being able to return to work at full capacity. After that her concerns focused on her financial future, particularly looking forward to her retirement. Having no partner and not wanting to bur-den or involve her children in her finances, her resources were limited. As a single person, she knew it was up to her to make sure she was on track. Without a plan, people panic or feel a sense of anxiety that may detract from their quality of life, pre- and post-retirement. Often, this worry is unnecessary.

Doris realised that although she had equity in her property her cash flow was tight. If she continued paying her mortgage as it was currently structured it was going to take her seventeen years, assuming she was able to keep up her mortgage repayments after her retirement in eight years' time.

Living in the minor dwelling was a good idea and suited her fine, but it wasn't enough to solve the problem of having to work until the mortgage was paid off, by which time Doris would have celebrated her seventy-eighth birthday!

Doris had made some good decisions, but these decisions in isolation were still not enough to give her a good retirement fund. She still needed to make a number of tweaks across the board to have the retirement she wanted. She needed a plan to give her clarity about what she needed to spend for her current lifestyle, and to reassure her she would still have a cash surplus. She needed to live the new plan and this meant restructuring her mortgage to allow her to build up a surplus to reduce her debt faster, and to save on interest. She also needed to maximise her tax deductions. Executed correctly, these simple changes were enough to achieve her goals, including her overseas travel.

When we started working together, we projected she would be mortgage-free in eight years. After three years she remains on track to achieve this. She has also enjoyed a lovely trip to Spain and is planning a trip to Alaska next year. If Doris can continue this plan until she is 68 she will have paid off her entire mortgage and will be able to retire ten years before she would originally have been able to. The rental income she receives from her former home will then sustain her lifestyle indefinitely.

CONCLUSION

Everybody's circumstances are different and their priorities and goals differ. People's lives change, too—sometimes for better, sometimes for worse. You must have flexibility and fluidity within your plan to either exploit or cope with those changes. Projections are one thing. Knowing what to do and when to do it and actually doing it are entirely different. Human nature usually makes us perform better when we are accountable.

If a plan is to succeed, it must be holistic. It is not just about your mortgage structure or, even, your bank accounts—all aspects of your finances need to be working in a coordinated way and at their optimum capacity to get the best results for your circumstances at any given time. Most importantly, you need to sustain performance and to do that you need to regularly check your progress against your projected outcomes. If you do not take control of your money, it will take control of you.

> **Money is only a tool—and a good workman never blames his tools.**

Chapter 7

Building momentum

It is one thing to start a journey. It's another thing to finish it. It's another thing altogether to finish it in the shortest possible time. Perseverance is key—getting the right results time and time again is what creates results. There are no short-cuts. Calvin Coolidge, the 30th President of the United States, said it best when he said:

> Nothing in the world can take the place of persistence. Talent will not; nothing is more common than unsuccessful men with talent. Genius will not; unrewarded genius is almost a proverb. Education will not; the world is full of educated derelicts. Persistence and determination alone are omnipotent.

KEEPING MOTIVATED

The most effective motivator is getting results, fast. Anyone would be prepared to make a concession on a day-to-day basis if they could see the benefits immediately. Likewise, there is nothing more demoralising than trying hard but not seeing a result. The beauty about managing your money without emotion and following a plan exactly as it is set out is that the results become a mathematical certainty—you simply can't stop yourself getting ahead faster. Too often people set the bar in the wrong place—either too low, where they sell themselves short, or too high, where they set themselves up for failure. The plan must be the perfect balance of stretching you to your capability without compromising your ability to achieve.

To do that you need to optimise all aspects of your financial life—that means every aspect of your finances, including your mortgage, bill payments, any investments you may have and your discretionary spending, will be working together to get the best possible results for you.

It is my experience that when all the elements of a plan are working together well, your past behaviour cannot dictate your capability. It is about not leaving anything to chance. Tweak everything a little bit, and you won't notice much change in the things you need to be doing, but you will notice a different outcome. For something to be sustainable the change has to be minute, but the impact huge.

CERTAINTY OF RESULTS

It is comforting to be able to rely wholly on an outcome, leaving nothing to chance. Looking forward to a promised result brings comfort and builds confidence. Equally, the surprise of an unexpected outcome, especially a negative one, creates confusion and despondency.

Nothing demonstrates this better than trying to lose weight. I know when I go on a strict diet and I follow the diet to the letter, drink eight glasses of water a day and exercise, but find when I hop on the scales at the end of the week that I haven't lost any weight or, worse still, I've gained weight, the despair is overwhelming. This is the same feeling many people get when they make a concession in one area of their spending or receive a payrise only to find their circumstances don't improve. That said, positive outcomes can also cause confusion, and if you do not make adjustments to the change in your circumstances, all too often the positive is not exploited to its full potential. (What really is the best thing to do with Great-aunt Maud's unexpected legacy to you?)

There are other parallels between trying to lose weight and trying to get ahead financially. This is one of the reasons I call myself a financial personal trainer! If you have tried to lose weight one week and not achieved anything—or even worse, put on weight—this can be a trigger to fall off the wagon well and truly. Instead of hitting the gym with more force many simply feel demoralised, and open and finish a packet of Tim Tams. It's emotional and illogical, but it still happens. Similar emotion affects people who've experienced a setback with money. If they feel like they have tried to stick to a budget but their circumstance does not feel any better or they are not seeing their debt reduce, then they get frustrated and demoralised. Instead of trying to save more, they hit the shops and splurge in frustration. The reaction, while emotional, is fairly common. The key to combating this is to ensure you get the results you expect and for the results to be sustainable.

GAINING MOMENTUM

To gain momentum you need to be on the move. With a good plan in place you will start to move in the right direction and that is when you want to gain momentum—not when you are going backwards! Remember these three steps to gaining and building momentum to achieve your goals:

- A good plan creates forward movement

- Movement builds momentum

- Momentum gets you to your goals.

In the beginning, moving in the right direction is the goal. After that, you can begin to gain momentum towards your financial goals and look to build speed. The first twelve weeks of any plan are the most critical. You have to get some runs on the board during this first quarter, otherwise you will lose interest and likely splurge on some unnecessary spending as a way of numbing the disappointment of your poor performance.

In building momentum, it is important you create an environment that empowers you and encourages you to behave the way you know you should. If you need to be accountable to someone in order to reach your potential, you need to find a reliable adviser that you trust and get on with, and can get results with. Personally, I have to check in with my financial coach every twelve weeks, as I have a way of rationalising anything and everything to myself, and I still sometimes lose sight of my longer-term goals.

HOW DO I STICK TO A PLAN?

To stick to a long-term financial plan, you need five things to be operating in unison:

- You must not be feeling deprived

- You need regular independent assessment of your potential as your circumstances change

- You need to get results

- You need to be accountable for the results you get

- You need to enjoy your lifestyle.

BEING ACCOUNTABLE

Being accountable to someone qualified and impartial increases the chances that you will reach your goals faster—fact. Many people happily use personal trainers and sports coaches to improve performance on the sports field, or in their day-to-day lives to help them keep their weight under control. Whether you are morbidly obese or an elite athlete, it is accepted that the support and guidance of a coach or personal trainer can help you do things better and faster. They help remove imaginary limitations and overcome real obstacles. They motivate you and keep emotion out of the equation. Good coaches can dance between dynamics of different money personalities and different financial goals in a relationship to get the best results for you both. For the same reasons, you should seek assistance with managing your finances to get further ahead faster.

A financial personal trainer is there to quantify your potential, down to the last dollar. If you are time-poor, their expertise can fast-track your progress. Not only will you get ahead faster, but you will also have a sounding-board for all your financial decisions. Someone impartial to discuss your finances with allows you to mitigate the effects of the money dynamic in your relationships and helps you suppress any irrational behaviour you may have around money. A financial personal trainer will also help you master any negative natural tendencies you may have as they cut to the chase without emotion. They'll keep you on track to achieve your goals as quickly as your circumstances allow. Getting ahead faster is not a desire reserved for the financially successful; it is an entitlement for all.

For people who do not want to work with a trainer, you have to have the ability to be honest and open about your finances. You could sit down with friends and set goals and check in with each other to make sure you are on track to achieve the goals. Have a budget party! Understand where your money is going. Do you have a cash surplus? What can you cut out to make this surplus bigger? Just remember that if you are struggling, it can often pay to speak to someone who is qualified and independent. You need to know your capability and often self-diagnosis sets the bar too low.

Even though I have written a comprehensive and effective program to help people get ahead faster than they would otherwise, I still apply the same principles to myself. We have paid off one mortgage and are about to pay off our second, but I still check in with my coach to make sure that we are living to our potential. Some of the stuff he tells me I already know, and some stuff I know but am not doing. Someone emotionally disconnected from my situation can see things that I can't because I'm too close to the woods and the trees do not always distinguish themselves, even to an arborist.

It is important, however, that your coach does not have anything to gain if you increase your debt or invest in a particular asset field. If this is the case they must, at the very least, disclose their conflict of interest. Conflicts of interest are rife in the world of finance, so be sure to ask any adviser directly if they know of any conflict of interest they may have.

CONCLUSION

To be financially successful, you need to be able to live a lifestyle you enjoy for as long as you live. Anyone who is doing well financially but has no retirement plan cannot say they are successful. You need to understand and apply financial smarts and know your financial capability. Considerable time needs to be taken to analyse, prepare, measure and tune your financial plan. If you are time-poor, delegate some of the preparation of your plan to someone more capable. But remember, no-one will ever care about your money as much as you, so you have a responsibility to do things the smartest way. The goal should be to manage your money so you can live a lifestyle you enjoy prior to and after retirement. If you manage it right, you will create the perfect balance—happiness within your means.

Special offer

I'm offering a discounted first meeting at my financial personal training company, enableMe, for anyone who would like help to get ahead faster after reading *The Perfect Balance*. In that meeting I will be able to ascertain where you are at financially, where you want to be, and whether it is possible to reach your goals faster than what you are currently on track to do. I will quantify your capability. It's up to you whether you decide to work with me from that point or not. But either way, following our first meeting you will know your capability; the next step is unlocking it. Visit <www.enableme.co.nz> to find out more.

Acknowledgements

The success of this book is due to a lot of people's hard work. It would never have been made if Angie hadn't meet Abba, and Abba hadn't introduced me to Nic. Without the help of Kathryn (my amazing editor) this book would still be languishing in the first chapters. Special thanks must be given to Paul and Justine, and Nigel and Peter. Your honesty and willingness to share your stories is the icing on the cake. Thank you.

The enableMe and the enableBusiness teams are always brilliant, but a special shout out must be made to Anne and Royden for being a much needed sounding-board during my brainstorming process.

Most importantly, though, I want to thank my family. My mum and dad, my husband Billy and my son Cameron. Without your love and support my life would be both impossible and irrelevant.

Appendix I—The five-step program

Follow these steps to ensure you are making progress towards finding the perfect balance. It's this simple:

- Understand the psychology of your spending

- Make sure you become financially literate

- Make a plan

- Stick to your plan

- Enjoy the journey and achieve your goals.

Don't let your genetics determine your financial potential. Understand your money personality (see Chapter 1) and work out how to mitigate it to increase your chances of success. If you are in a relationship and you understand your partner's spending habits, and your partner understands yours, and you work together to mitigate any conflict around money issues, it should be impossible for you to fail.

Understand the psychology of your spending.

Learn the rules of money (see Chapter 3) and apply them to your unique circumstances to get ahead faster. Sadly, New Zealand has one of the lowest levels of financial literacy in the developed world. Even many of our successful businesspeople don't know how to manage their personal money. They do not know if they are coming or going. If they are coming they have no idea where they have come from, and if they are going they don't always have a clear idea of where they are going.

Make sure you become financially literate.

Develop a plan to make sure you are doing things smarter—as smartly as you possibly can. I believe that if I cannot radically improve the financial position of a client beyond where it is when I meet them then either I have missed something or I'm not trying hard enough!

I aim to optimise people's positions and empower them to stretch themselves as they reach for and achieve goals that would have seemed impossible to them before we began working together.

Make a plan.

It's important to continually review your circumstances. If you do not have time to do this—it does take time— get someone impartial to do this for you. Small slippages can add up to big numbers over time if left unchecked. Do not disrespect the humble 10-cent coin. With nine more it becomes a dollar.

The key to every successful financial plan is to spend less than you earn so that you can repay any debt you have as quickly as possible. After that, you can save for your future, which can be painted with whatever colours you want.

> **Stick to your plan.**

Once you have a written plan, be accountable to it. Have it fluid enough so that curve balls can be absorbed and the numbers can change as circumstances change; for example, if you get a payrise, you should be getting ahead faster. Be accountable to someone, somewhere, who is qualified to comment and challenge you and your assumptions.

> **Enjoy the journey and achieve your goals.**

Appendix II—Financial compatibility questionnaire

Money is one of the most common sources of tension in relationships. If this is true for you and your relationship, the first thing you need to do is talk to your partner and work through the questionnaire below. This can also be useful if you are at date night two and you want to know if you guys are going to mesh financially! The questionnaire below assesses compatibility in isolation. Compatibility is not a measure of financial success, but in most instances it is a good place to start.

INSTRUCTIONS

1. Answer the questions below Yes/Agree or No/Disagree.
   Yes = 1
   No = 0
2. Complete the questionnaire for yourself and tally your score.
3. Next, complete the questionnaire from your partner's point of view, i.e. based on your perception of their relationship with money.
4. Have your partner complete the test on the same basis as above and tally their respective scores.

5 Compare their answers to the questions with your own.

Yes/No	You	Your partner
Are you a shopper?		
Are you a saver?		
Do you keep your finances separate?		
Are you an emotional spender?		
Do you manage the household's finances?		
Are you tight in your day-to-day spending?		
Do you use your credit card for day-to-day purchases?		
Do you research big purchases before buying?		
Are you an impulse buyer of small items?		
Do you consult each other for bigger purchases?		
Do you feel entitled to annual holidays, even if you can't pay for them with cash?		
Do you have champagne taste on a beer budget?		
Do you speak openly and regularly with each other about money?		
Do you share future financial goals?		

Agree/Disagree	You	Your partner
If one partner earns more than the other, they're entitled to spend more.		
If I receive a bonus it should be mine to spend.		
I look at my bank balances often and know that my card will be declined before it happens.		
If I receive a bonus it should be a reward to spend as we please, and should not go towards the general running of the household or repaying debt.		
Our kids should not have to live to a budget or go without anything.		
Our children should not be aware of our financial position.		
I believe a budget creates freedom to spend, not restriction.		
Our kids cost us too much and we need to say no to some of their spending behaviour.		
The best way to help our children financially is to give them what they need as they need it.		
We have clear financial goals, and plan to achieve them.		
I have a budget but don't stick to it.		
I have accepted that I am not good with money and never will be.		

Because I earn more than most, I feel that I should be more generous with my friends and family.		
We often disagree on what we spend our money on.		
I am happy to be told what to spend money on.		
I trust my partner to make all the financial decisions for us.		
I believe it is important to plan for the longer term.		
I am self-employed and do not believe I can project my earnings.		
Tallied results		

© enable Me Ltd

MEASURING YOUR RESULTS

This test assesses two areas. First, it highlights the perception you and your partner have of each other with regard to money. Compare how you answered each question when answering from your partner's point of view versus how they actually answered it. Are there any differences? If there are, this is the first problem that needs to be addressed. It is not unusual to see yourself differently from the way your partner perceives you. Discuss any differences and agree on what the appropriate answer should be. If you cannot agree on a point (which is possible a red flag), then attribute 0.5 to that question.

Re-tally your score based on any adjustments following your discussion. This will give you the basis of determining your actual compatibility.

Compare your updated score with that of your partner, and calculate the difference between your scores. Refer to the table below to diagnose where you sit on the compatibility scale.

Difference between scores	
0–2	You and your partner are very compatible and money is not likely to be a major stress in your relationship. Although you may have different money personalities, the mix of strengths looks like a good base on which to build your financial success, provided you share the same financial goals.
	Be aware, though, that it is possible to be compatible with money but still go nowhere. For example, this is could be the case if you are both shoppers. Compatibility does not immediately translate to increased financial capability, but it does position you well.
3–5	This difference indicates that you have different attitudes regarding money management in a number of areas, which is likely to be creating some tension in your relationship. While it is recommended that you sit down and discuss these issues, the discussion could become heated and personal. You might need to engage an impartial third party if you are committed to working towards a better endgame and do not want the emotional baggage and conflict along the way.

	People in this category often resolve their existing differences once they share the same financial goals and are making sustainable progress towards them. While you and your partner are possibly not as compatible as some, this difference need not hold you back financially—and you have identified the potholes you might have to deal with along the way.
6–11	This difference clearly highlights that you have a number of attitude differences regarding money, although not an insurmountable one. You probably feel the strain of these in your relationship, and they need to be resolved before money matters create tension in other facets of your life, and before you can head towards financial success. Remember, money is indirectly linked to most areas of life, so if you do not have a healthy synergy working, then the impact will be far-reaching. Money is important and you must set aside some specific time to work through the issues, and you may wish to consider getting some relationship coaching to help you through this.

While you may be coming at the issues from different perspectives, it usually pays to focus on your common goals. Once you agree what goals you are working towards and your individual requirements, if you still need some guidance then a good financial coach can help you tailor a plan so that everyone gets what they need individually and less emphasis is placed on each other's behaviour. |

6–11 (cont.)	When you have a workable and objective financial plan that you both have contributed to, no-one needs to become the financial police. This helps remove the emotion around money that might otherwise lead to conflict.
12 +	Hang up your gloves now . . . Only kidding. But you do have different attitudes towards money and you are going to have to do a lot of work to resolve potential conflicts in this area before you even think about longer-term financial success. We highly recommend that you involve a third party who can be objective and provide the necessary tools, free of emotion, to get you to a point of agreement, which is the first step to sustainable financial success. I have worked with many couples, some of whom were polar opposites of each other. Their coping mechanisms were either serious conflict or disengaging themselves from reality. Neither option will work for the long term. If you are committed to the relationship, keep working on these issues, otherwise money matters may tear your relationship apart.

© enable Me Ltd

Everyone has a relationship with money. When you combine your attitude to money with your partner's approach it can end in tears if you are not aware of each other's natural tendencies, and how to exploit the positives and manage the weaknesses.

Being compatible indicates a good base to work from, provided you share the same future financial goals. That said, compatibility in isolation counts for little (especially if you are both shoppers). There are other tools and skills that need to be mastered to ensure financial success is realised.

By the way, the shopper-and-saver combo is common and need not be a barrier to financial success, provided you both appreciate the roles you need to play.

Appendix III—Financial assessment template

Use this template to figure out where you are financially at the present time. Part 1 will help you understand the money you have coming in; Part 2 breaks down your current assets and liabilities; and Part 3 is a spending analysis that you can use to figure out where your money's going, and where you can make changes to start getting ahead.

PART 1—YOUR INCOME

INCOME

Net per annum

Name [   ]

Annual $
(after tax)

Source of income

Type of income

Total _____

Name [   ]

Type of income

Total _____

Income totals	Net per annum
Person 1	
Person 2	
Joint TOTAL	

© enable Me Ltd

PART 2—YOUR FINANCIAL POSITION

Assets—Property

Property address	Owned by	Purchased when	For how much	Current value
			Current value total:	$

Total property assets

© enable Me Ltd

Current mortgage structure

Which bank	Fixed or floating/for how long	Comes off fixed rate when	At what interest rate	Monthly repayment	Current balance
Total mortgage debt				Current debt total:	$

Net property assets (Current value total LESS current debt total)

$

© enable Me Ltd

Other assets

	Value
Car (1)	
Car (2)	
Motorbike	
Caravan	
Boat	
Savings	
Superannuation	
KiwiSaver	
Shares	
Bonus bonds	
Investments	
Term deposits	
TOTAL OTHER ASSETS	**$**

Other liabilities

Details (e.g. credit cards, hire-puchase car loan)	Interest rate	Card limit	Monthly payment	Amount owing
TOTAL AMOUNT OWING				$

Total other assets from p. 214 $

Total amount owing   – $

Total net other assets (other assets less amount owing)   = $

Total net property assets (from p. 213) $

Total net other assets (from above)   + $

Sum = total wealth   = $

PART 3—YOUR OUTGOINGS

	Monthly amount	Current annual
Accommodation		
Cleaner	x12	
Furniture and homewares	x12	
Gardening (lawns, garden bin)	x12	
House maintenance	x12	
Landscaping	x12	
Mortgage	x12	
Rates (water, land, regional)	x12	
Rent	x12	
Whitegoods and electrical	x12	
Other (e.g. body corporate fees)	x12	
Subtotal 1		$
Basic living costs		
Clothes, shoes (including dry-cleaning)	x12	
Electricity/gas	x12	
Food and household shopping	x12	
Internet	x12	
Mobile phones	x12	
Alarm	x12	
Firewood	x12	
Subtotal 2		

	Monthly amount	Current annual
Children, education, family costs		
Day care	x12	
Babysitting	x12	
Children's clothes	x12	
School extras (trips, etc.)	x12	
School fees	x12	
School uniforms	x12	
Tertiary education fees	x12	
Text books, stationery	x12	
Tuition/activities	x12	
Contributions to other family	x12	
	Subtotal 3	
Car, vehicle expenses		
Boat/campervan	x12	
Boat/campervan insurance	x12	
Boat/campervan maintenance	x12	
Maintenance	x12	
Parking	x12	
Petrol	x12	
Registration and WOF	x12	
Taxis, public transport	x12	
Tyre replacement	x12	
AA membership	x12	
	Subtotal 4	

	Monthly amount	Current annual
Financial		
Bank fees	x12	
Car insurance	x12	
Child support payments	x12	
Contents insurance	x12	
Credit card repayments	x12	
House insurance	x12	
Investment/savings	x12	
Life insurance	x12	
Medical insurance	x12	
Other (e.g. professional fees)	x12	
Other (e.g. ongoing support)	x12	
Other (e.g. property top-up)	x12	
	Subtotal 5	
Medical		
Chemist and prescriptions	x12	
Dentist	x12	
Doctor	x12	
Optometrist	x12	
Podiatrist	x12	
Naturopath	x12	
	Subtotal 6	

	Monthly amount	Current annual
Discretionary		
Alcohol	x12	
Annual holidays	x12	
Bars, clubs, pubs	x12	
Birthday presents	x12	
Books and magazines	x12	
Christmas presents	x12	
Church, tithing	x12	
Cigarettes	x12	
Donations	x12	
DVDs	x12	
Easter	x12	
Guy Fawkes	x12	
Hairdresser	x12	
Hobbies	x12	
Make-up, toiletries	x12	
Memberships (e.g. gym)	x12	
Movies	x12	
Music	x12	
Newspapers	x12	
Pet costs	x12	
Restaurants and cafes	x12	
Short breaks/weekends	x12	
Sky TV	x12	
Special events/outings	x12	
Sports	x12	

	Monthly amount		Current annual
TAB, casino, lotto		x12	
Takeaways		x12	
Vet		x12	
Work lunch		x12	
Dog registration		x12	
Coffees		x12	
Other		x12	
		Subtotal 7	

Total expenses	Add subtotals 1-7		$
Total net income (from page 211)			$
Total expenses (from above)		–	$
Initial surplus / deficit	(Total net income LESS total expenses)	=	$

If your total net income is greater than your total expenses, you have a surplus.

If your total expenses are greater than your total net income, you have a deficit.

Notes

1. There are two key assumptions with this: one, that the market hasn't changed, and two, that the business is not likely to improve. If you are unsure of the answers to these questions it would pay to speak to a financial analyst or someone who can give you an impartial opinion.

2. See Paul Rogers, 'The Cognitive Psychology of Lottery Gambling' in the *Journal of Gambling Studies*, vol. 14, no. 2, December 1998, pp. 111–134, and Jason Zweig, 'Your Money and Your Brain: Humankind evolved to seek rewards and avoid risks but not to invest wisely' in *Money Magazine*, September 2007, pp. 104–109.

3. See Amos Tversky and Daniel Kahneman, 'Loss Aversion in Riskless Choice: A reference-dependent model' in *The Quarterly Journal of Economics*, vol. 106, no. 4, November 1991, pp. 1039–1061; www.SixWise.com, 'The Six Most Feared but Least Likely Causes of Death', accessed 15 May 2012, <www.sixwise.com/newsletters/05/07/13/the-six-most-feared-but-least-likely-causes-of-death.htm>; Katie Moisse, 'What Happens in The Amygdala: Damage to brain's decision-making area may encourage dicey gambles', accessed 10 April 2012, <www.scientificamerican.com/article.cfm?id=amygdala-loss-aversion>; and Simon Gächter, Eric J. Johnson and Andreas Herrmann, 'Individual-Level Loss Aversion in Riskless and Risky Choices', IZA Discussion Paper No. 2961, Institute for the Study of Labor, Bonn, July 2007.

4. Jane Spencer, 'Lessons from the Brain-Damaged Investor' in *The Wall Street Journal*, 21 July 2005, p. 40.

5. See Jason Zweig, 'Your Money and Your Brain: Humankind evolved to seek rewards and avoid risks but not to invest wisely' in *Money Magazine*, September 2007, pp. 104–109; Sarah Lipoff, 'Peer Pressure and the Young Adult's Brain', accessed 12 March 2012, <www.funderstanding.com/child-development/peer-pressure-and-the-young-adults-brain>; and Laurence Steinberg, 'Risk Taking in Adolescence: New perspectives from brain and behavioural science' in *Current Directions in Psychological Science*, vol. 16, no. 2, April 2007, pp. 55–59.

6. MP Dunleavey, '5 Steps to Escaping Your Money Trap', accessed 18 May 2012, <http://web.archive.org/web/20090620180741/http://articles.moneycentral.msn.com/SavingandDebt/ManageDebt/5-steps-to-escaping-your-money-trap.aspx>

7. Dan Stone, Ben Wier and Stephanie M. Bryant, 'Does Financial Literacy Contribute to Happiness?' in *The CPA Journal*, vol. 77, no. 9, September 2007, accessed 16 April 2012, <www.nysscpa.org/cpajournal/2007/907/perspectives/p6.htm>.

8. Sonya Lyubomirsky, *The How of Happiness: A new approach to getting the life you want*, Penguin Group, New York, 2008.
9. Dan Stone, Ben Wier and Stephanie M. Bryant, 'Does Financial Literacy Contribute to Happiness?' in *The CPA Journal*, vol. 77, no. 9, September 2007, accessed 16 April 2012, <www.nysscpa.org/cpajournal/2007/907/perspectives/p6.htm>.
10. Dan N. Stone, Ben Wier and Stephanie M. Bryant, 'Reducing Materialism through Financial Literacy' in *The CPA Journal*, vol. 78, no. 2, February 2008, accessed 16 April 2012, <www.nysscpa.org/cpajournal/2008/208/perspectives/p12.htm>.
11. Australia and New Zealand Banking Group, 'ANZ Survey of Adult Financial Literacy in Australia', ANZ Banking Group Limited, November 2005.
12. Oliver James, *Affluenza: How to be successful and stay sane*, Vermillion, London, 2007.
13. These findings appeared in Priya Raghubir and Joydeep Srivastava, 'Monopoly money: The effect of payment coupling and form on spending behaviour' in the *Journal of Experimental Psychology: Applied*, vol. 14, no. 3, September 2008, pp. 213–225.
14. Thomas J. Stanley and William D. Danko, *The Millionaire Next Door: The surprising secrets of America's wealthy*, HarperBusiness, Pymble, 1998, pp. 141–210.
15. Neale S. Godfrey and Carolina Edwards, *Money Doesn't Grow on Trees: A parent's guide to raising financially responsible children*, with a revision by Tad Richards, Fireside Books, Simon & Schuster, New York, 2006.
16. Data used to create this graph courtesy of Terralink International Limited, Quotable Value Limited and Statistics New Zealand.
17. Donald J. Trump and Meredith McIver, *Trump: How to Get Rich*, Random House, New York, 2004, p. 102.
18. These figures are taken from an online poll conducted by the National Foundation for Credit Counseling in the US, cited by Sheryl Nance-Nash in '1 in 4 Spouses is Willing to Cheat . . . Financially', accessed 19 April 2012, <www.dailyfinance.com/2011/10/03/1-in-4-spouses-is-willing-to-cheat-financially>.